SIMPLY SCANDINAVIAN

SIMPLY SCANDINAVIAN

TRINE HAHNEMANN

Cook and Eat the Easy Way,
with Simple and Satisfying Scandi Recipes

Hardie Grant

QUADRILLE

CONTENTS

INTRODUCTION

I am not very zen. I am always on the move. Action is my therapy, my way to solve problems. Of course, I also need to breathe and be present in my life, so that I don't rush through every experience, good or bad. But the moments in which I forget everything and am present are few, fleeting and hard to grasp. Occasionally, the scent of food in the hallway will bring back a childhood memory, or when picking herbs in my front yard, their aromas will take me somewhere unexpected. These moments are like those mornings on my father's boat, when I would go ashore and the sound of the wind would make me stop and smile to myself, a smile of recognition: I am here.

However, the place where I reliably find order and can always live in the moment is the kitchen. It is when I am cooking and immersing myself in the creative process that my body takes over my mind and makes me forget. Most of the time, I need to keep it simple and simply cook what I feel is needed. The other moments when I can always find my inner calm are when I set my mind to what it is that I want to cook, the sparking of my creativity that will lead, later, to the joy of eating what I have made.

Humanity, collectively, has been under a lot of stress in recent years. Most people know what the covid crisis has meant to the hospitality industry, in particular. I am still in shock over what happened. Literally millions of restaurateurs and food business owners around the world – myself included – were under huge pressure; the money was pouring out daily. The not-knowing was the biggest challenge, we all had to make strategic decisions with no real idea about the future or what would be our new normal.

However, out beyond the chaos there was still always cooking, and people, and the belief that life would resume one day.

You can do a lot to try to control your stress levels, whether that be yoga, long walks, spending time in nature, breathing techniques and the practice of mindfulness. But my best de-stresser is – and has always been – cooking. Even in the craziest situations I can turn around, go into the kitchen and find myself in another zone. I make myself a cup of tea, get my apron on and fetch my big wooden chopping board with its burns and scratches. It has been the basis of more than twenty years of cooking and some twenty or more cookbooks! I get my knives out, open the refrigerator and gather whatever vegetables I have. I look into my spice drawer and move around the jars and tubs until the right pot of something speaks to me. I get out flour, eggs and sugar and start baking. Then I lose myself in the moment.

Velbekommen

Trine Hahnemann

DAILY COMFORT FOOD

Eating is about much more than simple survival in my part of the world. It is deep-rooted in our Scandinavian culture that food can give us comfort, too. We depend on food emotionally, as well as merely biologically. Food – or even the idea of food – soothes us and gives us a break from the daily grind.

When you know you've got a couple of hours of hard graft ahead of you in front of the computer to meet a deadline, you fetch yourself a coffee and a bun with butter and jam, sit down at your desk, sip your coffee and enjoy your bun. That feeling you get from the crumbly bun and steaming coffee, that small release, counters the stress and busy-ness: it is pure comfort. There is nothing wrong in looking for comfort; it's human. I strongly believe that – at times like those – the brain is not only asking for sugar, it is actively trying to divert you, to give you a break. To remind you that you, too, matter.

I find my longing for comfort food is connected both to my mood and to the seasons. On a rainy day, I might yearn for a spicy warming soup; on a weekend hosting guests I know a roast is the right choice, something for us to take our time over, acknowledging the ritual and anchoring ourselves to a tradition that give us comfort. In the summer, I feel an urgent need for fatty fish: my body is telling me something, it knows before my brain does that the fish will give me comfort. Or, after a very busy day at work where I haven't had time to eat much, I come home longing for hearty pasta, such as my Winter Veggie Carbonara on page 18.

If it is cold outside, and I need the hygge to spread all over my house in the evening, I will cook Meatballs and Creamy Cavolo Nero (see page 36). On those evenings, even if I am cooking, talking to my husband, listening to the news on the radio, answering a text on the phone, there will always be a fleeting moment where I think about my family, because those meatballs connect all the past generations to those that are yet to come. And that's the definition of comfort.

HEARTY, HEALTHY
WINTER BREAKFAST

In wintertime, I like to get up early to enjoy the dark, cold mornings. I make myself tea, light all the candles, sit down in the dark and write. After a couple of hours, it is time for breakfast, so I cook a hearty meal of eggs and greens as the sun starts to rise.

SERVES 4

10 eggs, lightly beaten
4 tbsp olive oil
1 onion, sliced
2 garlic cloves, chopped
1 red chilli, sliced
400g (14oz) flower sprouts (kalettes), or cavolo
    nero leaves (coarse ribs removed), well washed
    and roughly chopped
4 slices of stale bread
sea salt flakes (kosher salt) and freshly ground
    black pepper

Whisk the eggs together with salt and pepper.

Heat 3 tbsp of the oil in a frying pan (skillet) and sauté the onion, garlic and chilli for a few minutes. Add the greens and sauté for 5 minutes, sprinkling with salt and pepper.

In another frying pan, toast the bread on both sides in the remaining 1 tbsp of oil.

Now add the eggs to the vegetables and fold together until the eggs are about to set, but still soft. Serve with the toasted bread.

SPICY SPINACH SOUP

This is easy to prepare and quick to cook. When it comes to the spicing, you can use your favourites or, if you don't want it spicy, leave out the chilli, season with nutmeg and serve with crème fraîche. Always remember that recipes are just guidelines intended to help improve your cooking, so use this as a base on top of which all kinds of variations can be made. You can use frozen spinach here, though that will make the soup a less vibrant colour.

SERVES 4–6

2 tsp coriander seeds
2 tsp cumin seeds
3 tbsp olive oil
2 onions, finely chopped
3 medium-large garlic cloves, chopped
2 green chillies, chopped, plus more (optional),
　to serve
200g (7oz) white basmati rice, rinsed thoroughly
　in cold water
2 litres (scant 2 quarts) vegetable stock
3 large bay leaves
1kg (2lb 4oz) spinach, rinsed thoroughly
　in cold water
juice of 1 lemon
freshly ground nutmeg
250g (9oz) 10 per cent fat (full-fat) Greek yogurt
2 spring onions (scallions), sliced
sea salt flakes (kosher salt) and freshly ground
　black pepper

Roast the coriander and cumin seeds in a dry pan over a medium heat for a few minutes, then grind them in a mortar and pestle or a spice grinder.

Heat the olive oil in a large saucepan and sauté the onions, garlic and chillies for a few minutes. Add the ground spices, rinsed rice, stock and bay leaves, bring to the boil, then reduce the heat and let it simmer for 15 minutes. Remove the bay leaves.

Now add the washed spinach. Don't worry – it will fit! – the spinach will decrease greatly in volume, but help it along by stirring and pressing it down into the soup every now and then. Let it simmer for another 5 minutes.

Turn off the heat and blitz the soup with a hand blender. Pour the soup into a clean saucepan and reheat it. Add the lemon juice and season to taste with nutmeg, salt and black pepper.

Serve in warmed bowls with Greek yogurt, spring onions and, if you like it even more spicy, a sprinkle more chilli.

SPINACH AND POTATO GRATIN

These days, supermarkets seem to shun big leafy winter spinach in favour of plastic bags of ready-to-eat baby spinach. The bagged stuff is useful when you need to cook in a hurry, but for this dish the hearty large-leaved spinach is best. If you can't get it fresh, use frozen spinach.

SERVES 4

600g (1lb 5oz) spinach (see recipe introduction)
1 tbsp olive oil
2 leeks, sliced and well washed (see page 30)
2 large garlic cloves, chopped
4 eggs
250ml (9fl oz) single (light) cream
1 tsp freshly grated nutmeg
5–6 medium baking potatoes, well scrubbed
2 tbsp salted butter, plus more for the dish
sea salt flakes (kosher salt) and freshly ground
    black pepper

Rinse the spinach thoroughly; it might take several washes until it is clean. Drain well. Wilt the spinach in the water clinging to its leaves in a large saucepan, then drain well again.

Heat the olive oil in a frying pan (skillet) and sauté the leeks and garlic over a medium heat for about 5 minutes. The leeks should turn translucent but not take on any colour. Turn off the heat and add the wilted spinach.

Lightly beat the eggs, cream and nutmeg in a bowl and season with salt and pepper, then fold into the spinach mixture and set aside.

Preheat the oven to 180°C/350°F/Gas Mark 4.

Cut the potatoes in slices as thin as you can, using a mandoline if you have one.

Butter a 30 x 25cm (12 x 10in) ovenproof dish. Arrange half the potatoes in it, in layers, making sure the slices overlap a little. Spread the spinach mixture on top. Arrange the remaining potatoes over the spinach, add the 2 tbsp of butter in small dots and sprinkle with salt and pepper.

Bake in the oven for 30 minutes, then serve right away.

WINTER
VEGGIE CARBONARA

I started making veggie carbonara when I wrote my book *Scandinavian Green*.
I have never been a big bacon or pancetta fan, so this is perfect for me, and my
family likes it, though I doubt they will ever give up the meaty original!

SERVES 4

1 courgette (zucchini)
200g (7oz) Brussels sprouts
4 eggs
200g (7oz) Parmesan cheese, finely grated
  (shredded)
4 tbsp olive oil
2 garlic cloves, chopped
75g (2¾oz) walnuts, chopped
500g (1lb 2oz) cappelletti pasta, or penne
sea salt flakes (kosher salt) and freshly ground
  black pepper

Start by slicing the courgette into roughly 5cm
(2in) batons, or 1cm (½in) half moons. Cut the
bases off the Brussels sprouts, then separate
the leaves, finely chopping the inner hearts.

Lightly beat the eggs in a bowl and mix with
half the Parmesan.

Heat the olive oil in a sauté pan, add the
garlic and walnuts and sauté for 2–3 minutes,
then add the courgette and sauté for a further
5 minutes. Add the Brussels sprouts and
sauté for a final 2–3 minutes.

Meanwhile, boil the pasta in salted water for
9 minutes.

Turn off the heat under the pan of vegetables,
making sure to keep the mix warm. When the
pasta is done, drain well and place it back into
the pot right away. Add the vegetables and
fold in, along with the egg mixture. Season to
taste with salt and a lot of pepper. Serve right
away with the remaining grated Parmesan.

FRIED MACKEREL WITH SHAKEN REDCURRANTS

It's a real Scandinavian tradition to eat sweet-and-sour pickled berries as a condiment with either fish, chicken or meat. The raw cured redcurrants here – *lingon sylt* – are a Danish classic with fried plaice, herring or mackerel, roasted chicken, or old-school braised beef. They have high acidity, which works well with rich fried fish, or heavier meats.

You will have to start the shaken redcurrants at least three days before you want to eat them.

SERVES 4

For the shaken redcurrants
500g (1lb 2oz) redcurrants, plus more to serve
250g (9oz) caster (superfine) sugar

For the mackerel
4 mackerel fillets
4 leeks, sliced in 10cm (4in) sections and
  well washed (see page 30)
1 tbsp salted butter
small bunch of dill, roughly chopped
sea salt flakes (kosher salt) and freshly ground
  black pepper

Rinse the redcurrants in cold water, place in a large rectangular dish, sprinkle with the sugar and fold the sugar gently into the berries.

Leave at room temperature, shaking the dish now and then, until the sugar has dissolved. It will take about 3 days. Then place in an airtight container and refrigerate. They will keep, refrigerated, for about 8 weeks.

Sprinkle the mackerel fillets with salt and pepper and let them rest for 30 minutes before frying.

Steam the leeks over simmering salted water for 5 minutes, or until just tender, then drain and keep warm.

Fry the mackerel in the butter for 2–3 minutes on each side. Serve with the leeks and shaken redcurrants, sprinkling the plates with fresh redcurrants and dill.

JERUSALEM ARTICHOKE, LEEK AND APPLE SOUP

A classic winter soup; in my part of the world, the season for soup starts in November. Plan a day ahead, by making a bread dough which can then rest overnight so, next day, you can bake bread to go with this. When the loaf is in the oven, prepare the soup. If Jerusalem artichokes (sunchokes) are hard to come by, or don't agree with you, replace them with any other root vegetable.

SERVES 4

1kg (2lb 4oz) Jerusalem artichokes (sunchokes), well scrubbed
2 apples, ideally Cox, or other tart (sharp) apples
2 tbsp sunflower or rapeseed oil, or other neutral-tasting vegetable oil
2 leeks, sliced and well washed (see page 30)
1.5 litres (1.5 quarts) water
5 thyme sprigs
3 bay leaves
1 tsp freshly ground nutmeg
1–2 tbsp apple cider vinegar
sea salt flakes (kosher salt) and freshly ground black pepper
handful of curly parsley leaves, to serve

For the croutons
3 slices of stale bread (I like sourdough croutons)
2 tbsp olive oil

Cut the Jerusalem artichokes into small cubes and the apples into big chunks.

Heat the oil in a sauté pan over a medium heat. Sauté the leeks until translucent but not browned, then add the artichokes, apples, water, thyme, bay leaves and some salt and pepper. Bring to the boil, then reduce the heat to medium and let it simmer for 30 minutes.

While the soup is simmering, make the croutons. Cut the bread into big cubes and fry them in the olive oil, turning, until all sides are golden brown. Tip on to a sheet of kitchen paper (paper towel) to drain.

Take the thyme sprigs and bay leaves out of the soup, then blitz it with a hand blender, seasoning with the nutmeg, vinegar and more salt and pepper.

Serve in warmed bowls, scattered with the croutons and parsley.

SPICED YELLOW BEETROOT SOUP

Beetroots (beets) are superfoods, really healthy as well as cheap and easily available. So a great-tasting, spicy beetroot soup is incredibly useful as part of the basic repertoire of our everyday cooking! I had an idea that this soup would be good, and it was, so I'm pleased to add it to my winter menu.

SERVES 4

1kg (2lb 4oz) yellow beetroots (beets),
   or any beetroot you have to hand
200g (7oz) potatoes
1 tsp coriander seeds
3 green cardamom pods
3 bay leaves
6–8 black peppercorns
1 onion, finely chopped
2 garlic cloves, finely chopped
1 red chilli, chopped
40g (1½oz) ginger, finely grated (shredded)
3 tbsp grapeseed oil
1.5 litres (1.5 quarts) vegetable stock
sea salt flakes (kosher salt) and freshly ground
   black pepper

To serve

250g (9oz) full-fat crème fraîche (optional)
small bunch of coriander (cilantro), or pea shoots,
   coarse stalks removed

Peel the beetroots and potatoes and chop them up roughly.

Roast the coriander seeds in a dry frying pan (skillet) for a few minutes, then grind them with a mortar and pestle or a spice grinder. Put the cardamom, bay leaves and peppercorns in a small muslin/cheesecloth bag (or robust spherical tea strainer) and tie it with kitchen string.

In a large saucepan, sauté the onion, garlic, chilli, ginger and ground coriander in the oil for a few minutes. Add the beetroots, potatoes, stock and spice bag and bring to the boil, then reduce the heat, cover and simmer for 45 minutes. Remove the spice bag.

Blitz the soup in a blender, or with a hand blender, until creamy and smooth. Place the soup in a clean saucepan, reheat it gently and season to taste with salt and pepper.

Serve in warmed bowls with spoons of crème fraîche, if you like, and sprinkled with coriander or pea shoots.

SALMON WITH BLACK AND WHITE CABBAGE

In the wintertime, I eat a lot of cabbage; it's healthy, there are lots of different kinds to choose from, and it's cheap! But the main reason is simple: I love cabbage. I eat it fried for breakfast with poached eggs, in a salad for lunch, and I'm always trying to come up with new recipes for dinner! This recipe came about one evening as I was rootling through my refrigerator wondering what to cook from what I had. It went down really well; I loved the combination.

SERVES 4

400g (14oz) salmon fillet
1 tsp fennel seeds, lightly crushed
200g (7oz) cavolo nero
200g (7oz) white cabbage
1 tbsp sunflower oil
sea salt flakes (kosher salt) and freshly ground
  black pepper

For the sauce
50g (½ stick) salted butter
1 shallot, finely chopped
1 tbsp capers
leaves from 4 tarragon sprigs
100g (3½oz) pomegranate seeds

Preheat the oven to 200°C/400°F/Gas Mark 6.

Place the salmon on a baking sheet or baking tray and sprinkle with the fennel seeds, salt and pepper. Bake for 8–12 minutes depending on thickness (thicker pieces will take longer).

Tear both types of cabbage into medium-sized pieces, removing the coarse stalks.

Now make the sauce. Melt the butter in a small saucepan, add the shallot and let it simmer for 3–4 minutes. Add the capers and tarragon leaves and let it simmer for another 2 minutes, seasoning to taste with salt and pepper. Turn the heat off.

Flash-fry all the cabbage in the oil in a frying pan over a high heat for a few minutes, sprinkling with salt and pepper. Place the cabbage in a serving dish. With a fork, break the salmon fillet up into small pieces and place it among the cabbage.

Spoon the sauce over the salmon and cabbage, sprinkle with the pomegranate seeds and serve right away.

BAKED ONIONS

This is almost not a recipe, but I need to broadcast as widely as possible the concept of eating onions as a main course instead of just as a condiment, or simply added to other dishes. Serve these with salad, bread or dal: a perfect dinner on those days when you're in need of comfort food. Or try them with Celeriac-Potato Patties with Parsley Pesto (see page 53).

SERVES 4

12 medium-sized onions
50ml (¼ cup) olive oil
10 thyme sprigs
sea salt flakes (kosher salt) and freshly ground
   black pepper

Preheat the oven to 200°C/400°F/Gas Mark 6.

Wash the onions thoroughly and cut them in half from the roots to the tips, keeping all the peel on.

Place on a baking tray brushed with a little oil, cut sides up. Brush the onions with oil, sprinkle with salt and pepper and place the thyme on top.

Bake for 30–45 minutes until golden brown; the time this takes depends on how fresh the onions are and how much water is in them; fresher onions will take longer to cook. Serve.

CURRIED GREEN WINTER STEW

Meals we make during the busy weekdays need to be easy, use few ingredients and have only a short cooking time so you can have dinner on the table quickly. So I am a big fan of this recipe, and I cook it often. Sometimes I add cream, sometimes not, and the Brussels sprouts can be replaced with other cruciferous vegetables, such as broccoli or cauliflower, or both. I also make this with aubergine (eggplant) and tomatoes, leaving out the cream and adding a dash of soy sauce.

You can double the quantities here to make enough for two days, meaning tomorrow's dinner becomes super-easy! I need to plan my weekly meals in this way, because, in my house, we cook every day.

SERVES 4

2 leeks
2 tbsp grapeseed oil, or other neutral-tasting vegetable oil
200g (7oz) Brussels sprouts, halved
3 tbsp Madras (medium) curry powder
2 garlic cloves, chopped
2 bay leaves
2 courgettes (zucchini), cut into chunks
100ml (scant ½ cup) water
200ml (generous ¾ cup) single (light) cream
2–3 tbsp lemon juice
sea salt flakes (kosher salt) and freshly ground black pepper
handful of coriander (cilantro), coarse stalks removed, to serve
cooked pearled spelt or barley, or rice, to serve

Cut the leeks into 1cm (½in) slices and rinse them in cold water. The easiest way to do this is to place them in a bowl of water and leave them there for a few minutes; the dirt will fall to the bottom. Then lift the leeks out of the water and drain in a colander.

Heat the oil in a large sauté pan for which you have a lid over a medium-high heat. Tip in the Brussels sprouts and cook until lightly charred, then add the curry powder, garlic and bay leaves and cook for 3–4 minutes. Now add the leeks, courgettes and water. Cover with a lid and let it simmer for 5 minutes. Take the lid off, add the cream and bring to the boil, seasoning with salt, pepper and the lemon juice.

Serve right away, scattered with the coriander, with cooked grains.

ROAST PORK LOIN IN VERMOUTH

Sometimes, Sundays call for a roast; I love pork, but the meat needs to be of the best quality.
So I bicycle to my favourite butcher in the centre of Copenhagen to buy a big pork loin. I ask for
the part close to the neck with the most fat, not too lean, as that way it makes for a juicier roast.
Pork is not butchered in the same way in different countries; some call this cut 'neck loin', others
'Boston butt'. Whatever its proper name where you live, describe the cut you want
to your butcher; they should know what you need.

SERVES 8

1 pork loin (see recipe introduction),
    1.35–1.8kg (3–4lb)
4 onions
20 sage leaves
10 thyme sprigs
4 garlic cloves, chopped
300ml (1¼ cups) dry white vermouth,
    or white wine
300ml (1¼ cups) water
200g (7oz) pearl barley
200g (7oz) green beans
2 tbsp olive oil
handful of flat-leaf parsley leaves, chopped
sea salt flakes (kosher salt) and freshly ground
    black pepper

Preheat the oven to 180°C/350°F/Gas Mark 4.

Brown all sides of the pork loin in a dry frying
pan (skillet), then sprinkle with salt and
pepper and place in a roasting tin. Cut the
onions into wedges, mix with the sage, thyme
and garlic and place around the pork loin in
the tin, then pour in the vermouth or wine
and the water.

Place in the oven and roast for 50 minutes.
Make sure there is liquid in the tin all the
time; if it runs dry, add more water.

Meanwhile, boil the barley in a saucepan of
water for 15–20 minutes, then drain and cover
to keep warm.

Trim the green beans and fry in the olive oil in
a frying pan (skillet) for 5 minutes, sprinkling
with salt and pepper.

Take the roast out and place on a carving
board, then slice it. I don't find there is usually
any need to rest it in this recipe.

Mix the barley into the pork juices, onions
and herbs in the tin, seasoning with salt and
pepper. Place the sliced pork on top, then the
green beans and parsley. Serve right away.

FRIKADELLER WITH SWEET AND SOUR CUCUMBER SALAD

This is so quintessentially Danish, but with a twist. *Frikadeller* are in the top ten most-cooked recipes in Denmark and every family has their own version; the discussion about which is the best meat to use for them will never end! I use a mix of minced (ground) pork and beef, adding vegetables to the raw mixture because it makes the meatballs light and juicy. If you don't eat red meat, you can use minced chicken instead of the pork and beef. Or, for a vegetarian version, grate a variety of root vegetables to replace the minced meat. However you choose to make these, they are good with Spiced Roast New Potato Salad on the side (see page 79).

SERVES 4

250g (9oz) minced (ground) pork
250g (9oz) minced (ground) beef
1 courgette (zucchini), grated (shredded)
1 onion, grated (shredded)
2 garlic cloves, grated (shredded)
1 tbsp chopped thyme leaves
3 eggs, lightly beaten
50g (1¾oz) breadcrumbs
3 tbsp plain (all-purpose) flour
50ml (¼ cup) sparkling water
50g (½ stick) salted butter
2 tbsp neutral-tasting vegetable oil

For the salad
250ml (1 cup) 5 per cent acid distilled vinegar
50ml (¼ cup) water
125g (4½oz) caster (superfine) sugar
1 tsp sea salt flakes (kosher salt)
1 tsp mustard seeds
1 tsp black peppercorns
2 large cucumbers
freshly ground black pepper

Start with the cucumber salad, because it needs to pickle for 30 minutes. Whisk together the vinegar, water and sugar. When all the sugar has dissolved, add the salt and some black pepper, along with the mustard seeds and peppercorns. Halve the cucumbers lengthways, scrape out the seeds with a teaspoon, then cut into half moons 5mm (¼in) thick. Place the cucumber in the brine, gently folding now and then, until ready to serve.

To make the meatballs, mix the minced meats, courgette, onion, garlic, thyme and eggs together and mix well. Fold in the breadcrumbs and flour and mix again. Lastly, mix in the sparkling water and season with salt and pepper.

Preheat the oven to 180°C/350°F/Gas Mark 4.

Melt the butter and oil in a frying pan (skillet). Use a spoon and your free hand to shape the meat mixture into medium-sized oval balls. Place in the butter and oil and fry on all sides until golden brown. Transfer to an ovenproof dish and bake in the oven for 10 minutes to finish cooking. Take the cucumber out of the brine (you can re-use the brine, so don't throw it away), and serve it in a bowl alongside the *frikadeller*.

MEATBALLS AND
CREAMY CAVOLO NERO

For me, meatballs are the ultimate comfort food. When it is cold and dark outside and I am low on batteries and I just need something that will really comfort me and give me energy, I turn to meatballs. I cook them in so many ways, but this is my newest recipe. Serve with boiled or mashed potatoes.

SERVES 4–6

For the meatballs
1 large courgette (zucchini), about 300g (10½oz)
400g (14oz) minced (ground) beef
1 onion, finely chopped
1 garlic clove, finely chopped
1 tbsp chopped thyme leaves
2 medium eggs, lightly beaten
4 tbsp plain (all-purpose) flour
2 tbsp small (not jumbo) rolled oats
100ml (scant ½ cup) sparking water
sea salt flakes (kosher salt) and freshly ground
   black pepper

For the sauce
1 tbsp salted butter
2 leeks, sliced into 2cm (¾in) pieces and well
   washed (see page 30)
100ml (scant ½ cup) white wine
200ml (generous ¾ cup) single (light) cream
1 tsp freshly grated nutmeg
200g (7oz) cavolo nero, coarse ribs removed,
   roughly chopped

Start by making the meatball mixture. Grate (shred) the courgette and place in a large mixing bowl. Add the minced meat, onion, garlic and thyme. Combine well, so the vegetables are mixed into the meat, then mix in the eggs. Now fold in the flour and oats, seasoning well with salt and pepper. Lastly, fold in the sparkling water.

Preheat the oven to 180°C/350°F/Gas Mark 4.

Shape the mixture into balls and place on a baking tray lined with baking parchment. Bake them in the oven for 25 minutes.

Melt the butter in a sauté pan and sauté the leeks for a few minutes, then pour in the white wine. Let it simmer for 5 minutes, then add the cream and let simmer again. Season to taste with salt, pepper and the nutmeg. Now wilt in the cavolo nero and let it simmer for a few minutes.

Place the creamy cavolo nero on a warmed platter and arrange the cooked meatballs on top.

CHICKEN BREASTS IN CURRY SAUCE WITH GRAPES

A recipe from my teens, when I cooked for 100 people at a boarding school every day for a year. I went to a very progressive boarding school, where students took part in everything; we learned about democracy and how we could make the world a more equal place. We cleaned, cooked and learned DIY, while discussing the best way to live in this world. I was on the kitchen team for a whole year and it was then that I learned to cook. This was on my menu a couple of times every month.

SERVES 4

200g (7oz) spring cabbage, or white cabbage
200g (7oz) green grapes
2 onions
2 chicken breasts
2 tbsp salted butter
4 tbsp Madras (medium) curry powder
100ml (scant ½ cup) water
200ml (generous ¾ cup) single (light) cream
sea salt flakes (kosher salt) and freshly ground
    black pepper

To serve (optional)
cooked rice, or other grains
gooseberry chutney, or another chutney

Cut the cabbage into 1cm (½in) slices and halve the grapes. Cut each onion into 4–6 wedges, depending on size. Cut each chicken breast into 3.

In a sauté pan, melt the butter, add the curry powder and let it simmer for a few minutes. Brown the chicken pieces on each side in the curry butter, then take out the chicken and set aside on a plate.

Now add the onions to the butter and sauté for 5 minutes. Return the chicken to the pan, pour in the water and the cream and add the grapes. Let it simmer for 5 minutes, seasoning with salt and pepper.

Now add the cabbage, mix it in and allow everything to simmer for a minute or two. Serve with rice and chutney.

BAVETTE WITH MY
SECRET DRESSING

I rarely eat red meat, so it is a real treat when I cook it for myself. One of my favourite cuts is bavette, or onglet, or hanger steak… this cut has many names. It is very easy to cook, just on a griddle pan (grill pan) or frying pan (skillet) for a few minutes on each side. It has a very meaty flavour with lots of sweetness and I only need a few bites for my meat craving to be satisfied for a long time to come. I serve it with 'my secret dressing'… thus named because a friend once called me and asked for the dressing recipe I had served at a dinner party. My answer was, 'Oh, it is my secret dressing,' mostly because I could not really remember what I had put in it! After that, I got the recipe together, and I give it to you here. The steak is good with baked potatoes, or Fermented Potato Chips and Skins with Herb Mayo (see page 56).

SERVES 4–6

600g (1lb 5oz) bavette steak, also known
    as onglet or hanger
200g (7oz) white cabbage

For the dressing
1 cucumber
1 egg yolk
1 very small garlic clove, finely grated (shredded)
2 tbsp lemon juice, plus more to taste
1 tbsp Dijon mustard
1 tsp honey
10 tarragon sprigs
50ml (¼ cup) extra virgin olive oil
1 tbsp capers
sea salt flakes (kosher salt) and freshly ground
    black pepper
leaves from a small bunch of basil, to serve

Start by preparing the dressing. Halve the cucumber lengthways, scrape the seeds out with a teaspoon, then cut it into very small cubes. Divide the cucumber into 2 portions. Combine the egg yolk, garlic, lemon juice, mustard, honey and tarragon, then blend them together with a hand blender, or in a food processor. Add the oil and some salt and pepper and blend again. Season to taste with salt, pepper and lemon juice, then fold in the capers and half the cucumber.

Get a griddle pan (grill pan) or frying pan (skillet) screaming hot. On the hot pan, sear the meat on both sides for 1–2 minutes to get a nice brown crust. Now sprinkle with salt and pepper and fry or grill it for a few more minutes. When done, remove it from the heat and let it rest for a few minutes.

Chop the white cabbage into ribbons and place it on a large serving dish with the remaining cucumber. Carve the meat into slices against the grain, so it won't be chewy, and place it on top of the cabbage. Drizzle the dressing over the meat, scatter with basil leaves and serve right away.

FISH PIE

The ultimate comfort food, but also light; this recipe manages to be creamy and filling without you having to take a nap afterwards, which can be the case with heavier meat dishes. It can be made with any fish, or also with the same weight of vegetables instead. This kind of pie will always do it for me when I'm in need of energy and comfort.

SERVES 6

800g (1lb 12oz) large potatoes, chopped into big chunks
100g (1 stick) salted butter, plus 3 tbsp, plus more for the dish
500g (1lb 2oz) firm white fish fillet, chopped into small pieces
300g (10½oz) raw prawns (shrimp), sustainably caught
10 white asparagus spears
10 green asparagus spears
2 shallots, finely chopped
200g (7oz) shelled fresh peas (garden peas)
5 dill sprigs, chopped
sea salt flakes (kosher salt) and freshly ground black pepper
leaves from 2–3 sprigs of flat-leaf parsley, chopped, to serve (optional)

Boil the potatoes in water until tender.

Butter a large ovenproof dish generously, then add the chopped fish and prawns in an even layer. Season with salt.

Snap the lower one-third of the white and green asparagus off, then peel the white asparagus until shiny and cut all the asparagus spears into 4cm (1½in) pieces. (The trimmings and peelings can be used in soup, see page 59.) Fry the shallots gently in a frying pan (skillet) in 1 tbsp of butter. Turn off the heat, add the asparagus, peas and dill, mix well and season with salt and pepper. Arrange the vegetable mixture on top of the fish.

Preheat the oven to 200°C/400°F/Gas Mark 6.

When the potatoes are cooked, drain them, reserving 100ml (scant ½ cup) of their cooking water. Mash the potatoes lightly together with the reserved cooking water and the 100g (1 stick) of butter, keeping the mash chunky. Season to taste with salt and pepper, then spread the mash over the pie filling and place the remaining 2 tbsp butter, in small dots, on top.

Bake for 30 minutes. Let it rest for a few minutes, then scatter with parsley and serve.

FEELING
GREEN

The way I eat has adapted throughout my life, either because of what produce is available where I am living, the food trends of the moment, how much money I have or how well-equipped my kitchen is. But one thing has remained constant: I have always eaten a lot of vegetables, even as a child. Steamed cabbage as my *mormor* (grandma) would cook it, slices of cucumber on rye bread, my father's 1970s stir-fry with beans and brown rice, over-cooked leeks with brown butter, or steamed cauliflower that fell apart if you so much as looked at it. Any creamy vegetable soup has always been a favourite of mine and so I learned early on to bake bread to go with it. If I was short of time, I'd make the bread with lots of yeast and only let it rise for 40 minutes, then bake it as flatbread with seeds and spices scattered on top.

Luckily for someone who adores vegetables, a lot has happened during my lifetime in the world of vegetable cookery; a small revolution, you could say. At the same time, my way of eating has changed gradually over the last decade or so and become even more vegetable centred. So this chapter truly reflects the way I eat every day.

Most of the recipes here came about in an unplanned way. I open my refrigerator, which is always full of seasonal produce bought from a local farm 40km (25 miles) from Copenhagen. I take it all out, consider it, then decide what I would like for dinner. If I hit on a new combination, I will write it down, then cook it again and make the ratios more precise: it becomes a recipe. At other (more random) times, I just cook everything I have and enjoy the result! When I get to the end of my weekly produce, I gather what's left and make a creamy vegetable soup.

In this chapter there are classic recipes I always return to, such as asparagus salad with beurre blanc, and celeriac-potato cakes, but there are also some of my new ideas: split pea patties with peperonata; vegetable tacos in which paper-thin kohlrabi slices take the place of tortillas; or making fermented potato chips and skins with herb mayo as a main course, with salads on the side.

I hope I can inspire you to make vegetables the centre of your plate and your appetite. The world needs us all to love them.

POTATO PANCAKES

A Norwegian tradition at weddings. In the old days, in small towns in Norway, all the women would gather together to make really big potato pancakes to be eaten at wedding breakfasts! This recipe takes a little planning because you need to prepare the potatoes the day before to allow their starch to settle, in order to be able to roll out the dough.

MAKES 10

For the pancakes
500g (1lb 2oz) peeled potatoes
50g (½ stick) salted butter
50g (1¾oz) full-fat crème fraîche
1 tsp sea salt flakes (kosher salt)
175g (6oz) plain (all-purpose) flour,
  plus more to dust
freshly ground black pepper

For the topping
200g (7oz) spinach
4 tomatoes
1 onion, sliced
1–2 tbsp salted butter
2–3 tbsp full-fat crème fraîche

The day before you want to make the pancakes, boil the potatoes until tender. Drain them, then pass through a potato ricer into a bowl and add the butter, crème fraîche and salt, with some pepper. Mix well, then cover and refrigerate overnight.

Next day, mix the flour into the potato mixture and divide the dough into 10. Roll each piece out on a floured work surface into a circle 12cm (4½in) in diameter. Cook each one in a dry frying pan (skillet), turning it once. You will know they are ready when they are light brown on both sides, which will take 2–3 minutes on each side.

For the topping, rinse the spinach in cold water and drain well; it may take several rinses to get it properly clean. Cut the tomatoes in half and discard the juice and seeds, then slice them. Sauté the onion in the butter until golden brown, then add the spinach and wilt it, seasoning to taste with salt and pepper. Turn the heat off, add the tomatoes and mix.

Serve the warm pancakes topped with the vegetables, with crème fraîche on the side.

SAVOURY WAFFLES
WITH CHANTERELLES

So deliciously fancy, but so simple. Serve these when you have people over for dinner. I change the topping according to my mood and the season; here is an autumnal version. In summer, serve the waffles with salad, in spring with asparagus, in winter with sautéed cabbage, and all year round for brunch with spinach and smoked salmon.

SERVES 4

250g (9oz) plain (all-purpose) flour
10g (¼oz) fresh yeast, or 3g (½ tsp) fast-action
  (instant) dried yeast
1 tsp sea salt flakes (kosher salt)
2 tsp freshly ground black pepper
225ml (scant 1 cup) whole milk
200ml (generous ¾ cup) buttermilk
3 eggs, lightly beaten
115g (1 stick) salted butter, melted, plus more
  to cook

For the topping

300g (10½oz) chanterelles
1 tbsp olive oil
1 tbsp salted butter, plus 1 tsp
1 garlic clove, finely chopped
leaves from 5 thyme sprigs
500g (1lb 2oz) spinach, rinsed well in cold water

For the chive cream

200g (7oz) full-fat cream cheese
100g (3½oz) full-fat Greek yogurt
3 tbsp finely chopped chives

Prepare the batter by mixing the flour, yeast, salt and pepper in a large mixing bowl.

In a second bowl, whisk the milk, buttermilk, eggs and melted butter together. Make a well in the dry mix and pour the wet mix into it gradually, whisking until smooth.

Brush the chanterelles with a dry brush, or wipe gently with a sheet of kitchen paper (paper towel) if needed. Do not rinse under water as they will become soggy.

To make the chive cream, in a mixing bowl beat the cream cheese with a fork to soften it. Fold in the yogurt and chives, then season to taste with salt and pepper.

Heat up your waffle iron according to the manufacturer's instructions and butter it well, then pour in the waffle batter and cook until crisp. Continue making waffles until all the batter has been used.

In a frying pan (skillet), heat the olive oil and 1 tbsp butter, then sauté the chanterelles with the garlic and thyme, seasoning to taste with salt and pepper. In a saucepan, wilt the washed spinach in the 1 tsp butter.

Serve the sautéed chanterelles and spinach with the baked waffles and chive cream.

ASPARAGUS SALAD WITH BEURRE BLANC

You can never go wrong with a classic sauce such as beurre blanc and it works brilliantly with white asparagus. Germans are famous for loving their *Spargel*; they even have festivals to celebrate it when the vegetable is in season. When I was growing up, asparagus was reserved for fine dining and a bit of a once-a-year experience, so I rarely tasted it, but really liked it when it was fresh and not overcooked. In Denmark, renowned farmer Søren Wiuff, from the northern part of Sjælland, grows white, violet and green spears. He has excellent soil for asparagus up there! The spears are so full of flavour and like nothing else I have tasted. I try to get my hands on some in the early summer, then eat it almost every day for the few short weeks it is in season.

Serve this on its own with a baguette, or boiled baby new potatoes (fingerlings).

SERVES 4

20–24 white asparagus spears
4 tbsp cress, or microgreens

For the beurre blanc
2 shallots, finely chopped
250ml (1 cup) white wine
250g (2 sticks plus 2 tbsp) salted butter, chilled
   and cut into cubes
sea salt flakes (kosher salt) and freshly ground
   black pepper

Peel the asparagus spears from the tips down; when they are a little shiny, you know you have removed enough peel. Snap off the lower one-third of the spears (you can use these trimmings for soup, see page 59).

Steam the trimmed asparagus over boiling water for 4–5 minutes.

Now make the beurre blanc: in a saucepan, boil the shallots in the wine for a few minutes, then add the cold butter cubes one at a time, whisking after each addition. Keep going until you have used all the butter; you'll have a smooth sauce. Make sure it does not boil, or it might split. Season to taste with salt and pepper.

Put the asparagus on a platter, pour over the beurre blanc and decorate with the cress or microgreens.

CELERIAC-POTATO PATTIES WITH PARSLEY PESTO

Before winter sets in and the Scandinavian soil has frozen solid, we dig up our root vegetables and store them to eat later in the winter. Most of these root vegetables are white, which in our region reflects the season's white landscapes, and its many days of clouded white sky. Accompany these patties with a crisp salad, if you like.

SERVES 4

250g (9oz) celeriac (celery root)
250g (9oz) potatoes
1 small onion, finely grated (shredded)
1 small garlic clove, finely grated (shredded)
2 tbsp plain (all-purpose) flour
50g (1¾oz) small (not jumbo) rolled oats
50g (1¾oz) sesame seeds
½ tsp freshly grated nutmeg
10 sage leaves, finely chopped
2 eggs, lightly beaten
50ml (¼ cup) grapeseed oil, or other
    neutral-tasting vegetable oil
sea salt flakes (kosher salt) and freshly ground
    black pepper

For the parsley pesto
50g (1¾oz) curly parsley
30g (1oz) hazelnuts
1 small garlic clove, finely grated (shredded)
1 tsp salted capers, rinsed and drained
150ml (generous ½ cup) grapeseed oil
2–3 tbsp lemon juice

Peel the celeriac and potatoes. Grate (shred) both vegetables, place in a mixing bowl and add the onion, garlic, flour, oats, sesame seeds, nutmeg and sage. Fold in the eggs and season with salt and pepper.

Set a frying pan (skillet) over a medium heat and add the oil. With a tablespoon, place a spoon of potato mixture in the oil, press it flat and fry for 5 minutes on each side. Repeat to form and fry all the mixture. You may need to do this in 2 batches, depending on the size of your pan, as you should not overcrowd the pan with patties.

Meanwhile, blend all the ingredients for the pesto in a food processor to a smooth paste, seasoning to taste with salt and pepper.

Serve the celeriac-potato patties with the parsley pesto.

VEGETABLE TACOS

I am going out on a limb here, writing a book about simple Scandinavian food while using miso(!), but this dish has become one of my staples, due to my sister, Sille Bjerrum, who is also a chef. She specializes in Japanese food and makes some of the best sushi I have ever tasted. Her dressings are also phenomenal and the dressing here is inspired by a miso dressing from her book *Simple Japanese*. Different food cultures and their ingredients may travel to Scandinavia and change with each cook who experiments with them, but the core of our food remains the same, because of our northern land and its weather. I like to serve this miso dressing with the local vegetables I eat every day.

SERVES 4

1 kohlrabi
2 carrots
1 cucumber
2 spring onions (scallions)
75g (2¾oz) cashew nuts
2–3 tbsp cress
2–3 tbsp finely chopped chives
  (optional but good!)

For the dressing
2 tbsp miso paste
1 tbsp soy sauce
1 tbsp honey
2 tbsp finely grated (shredded) ginger
1 tbsp grainy mustard
2 tbsp lemon juice, plus more to taste
2–3 tbsp water
2 tbsp grapeseed oil
freshly ground black pepper

Start with making the dressing: in a mixing bowl, mix the miso, soy sauce, honey, ginger, mustard, lemon juice and water to a smooth paste. Gradually whisk in the oil, season to taste with pepper and a touch more lemon juice, if you like.

Wash the kohlrabi and slice into super-thin slices, using a mandoline if you have one. Cut the carrots, cucumber and spring onions into 5–6cm (2–2¼in) strips. Toast the cashew nuts in a dry frying pan (skillet), then cool them down and chop.

Fold the kohlrabi slices into taco-like shapes. In their centres, place a bit of each of the carrots, cucumber and spring onions, drizzle with the miso dressing and top with the cashews, cress and chives, if you like. Serve right away.

FERMENTED POTATO CHIPS AND SKINS WITH HERB MAYO

Making these takes some planning, because the potatoes need to ferment for three days. This recipe is also in my book *Scandinavian Green*, but I think the chips (fries) are so good – with loads more flavour and crispness than regular chips – that I need to repeat it here! You will need two large jars.

SERVES 4

1.5 litres (1.5 quarts) water
10g (2 tsp) fine sea salt without added iodine, to be safe for fermentation
1kg (2lb 4oz) large floury potatoes
2 large white cabbage leaves
2 litres (scant 2 quarts) sunflower oil

For the mayo
2 egg yolks
2 tbsp white wine vinegar
1 tsp Dijon mustard
2 tbsp chopped tarragon leaves
1 tbsp chopped chives
6 tbsp chopped parsley leaves
200ml (generous ¾ cup) grapeseed oil, or other neutral-tasting vegetable oil
sea salt flakes (kosher salt) and freshly ground black pepper

Whisk the water and salt together. Scrub the potatoes, then cut one on all sides so you have a big, peel-free potato cube. Put the slices with skins to one side. Cut the potato cube lengthways into 1cm (½in) slices. Cut each slice into thick chips (fries) and rinse in a colander. Repeat to prepare all the potatoes. Place the skinless potato chips in a jar and the potato skins in another. Pour the salty water over both and cover the top of each with a cabbage leaf. Close the jars, then each day open them briefly, to 'burp' them. After 3 days, they will be ready.

To make the mayo, put the egg yolks, vinegar and mustard in a food processor, season with salt and pepper and blend for 5 minutes. Add all the herbs and blend again. Now add the oil, trickling it in while blending, until you have used it all. Season to taste and set aside.

Preheat the oven to 200°C/400°F/Gas Mark 6. Drain the potatoes, then pat them dry with a tea (dish) towel. Put the potato skins in a roasting tray lined with baking parchment and toss with some oil. Bake for 30 minutes.

In a pan at least 8cm (3¼in) deep, heat the oil to 120°C (250°F) and fry the chips in batches for 5 minutes until just cooked through. Remove, drain and pat dry. When ready to eat, heat the oil to 160°C (325°F) and add the chips again. Fry in batches until crisp and golden, then drain, season and serve with the potato skins and mayo.

WHITE ASPARAGUS SOUP

This soup is ivory pale with an almost polished finish and little crunchy pieces of white asparagus floating around to give you a nice surprise. It is the ultimate pleasure, one of those dishes that is eaten in a sudden hush, as everyone concentrates on the deliciousness.

SERVES 4

800g (1lb 12oz) white asparagus spears
50g (scant ½ stick) salted butter
2 shallots, chopped
1 celery stick, sliced
4 tbsp plain (all-purpose) flour
300ml (1¼ cups) dry white wine
2 bay leaves
1.2 litres (1.2 quarts) vegetable stock
200ml (generous ¾ cup) single (light) cream
sea salt flakes (kosher salt) and freshly ground
    black pepper
leaves from 2–3 chervil sprigs, chopped, to serve

Peel the asparagus spears from the tips down; when they are a little shiny, you know you have removed enough peel. Snap off the lower one-third of the spears. Reserve these end pieces and the peelings. Set aside the peeled asparagus spears.

Melt the butter in a saucepan, add the shallots and celery and sauté for a few minutes before adding the flour. Stir well, then add the white wine and stir again until you have a thick, smooth paste. Add the white asparagus end pieces and peelings and the bay leaves.

Gradually stir in the stock, bring to the boil, then reduce the heat, add salt and pepper and let the soup simmer for 30 minutes.

After 30 minutes, pass the soup through a sieve into a bowl and discard the vegetables. Pour the soup back into a clean saucepan and bring slowly to the boil. Cut the asparagus spears you set aside into 1cm (½in) slices on an angle. Stir them into the soup along with the cream and let it simmer for 5 minutes, then season to taste with salt and pepper.

Serve hot, scattered with chervil.

NORDIC GUACAMOLE

Green split peas are a wonderful pulse that we simply ought to eat; right now, we mostly use them as animal feed. When I think of the big changes that the future will bring, it is clear to me that we need to change the way we eat to a greener diet. What does that mean? First and foremost: less meat and more vegetables, pulses and grains. So, we need lots more new recipes for how to eat pulses. This is one of my recent favourites, inspired by guacamole, and it is far more versatile than just a dip, though it is of course excellent with bread and leaves for dipping. It has lots of flavours, is great in a sandwich with chips (fries) on the side, on rye bread with sliced tomatoes, or served with cooked vegetables, crudités and crusty bread.

SERVES 8

200g (7oz) green split peas
2 tsp coriander seeds
1 green chilli, finely chopped
1 small garlic clove, finely grated (shredded)
2 tsp finely grated (shredded) ginger
1 spring onion (scallion), sliced, plus more
   to serve
3 tbsp grapeseed oil
3 tbsp lime juice, plus more to taste
coriander leaves (cilantro), to serve
sea salt flakes (kosher salt) and freshly ground
   black pepper

The night before you want to serve the dip, soak the peas in a large bowl, generously covered with water.

The next day, drain the peas, then boil them in fresh water for 12 minutes. Drain once more – this time reserving 3–4 tbsp of the cooking water – and leave to cool.

Pulse the cooled peas in a food processor, but make sure they do not turn into a paste; the mixture should be crumbly, like breadcrumbs.

Toast the coriander seeds in a hot dry frying pan (skillet) for 1 minute, then grind in a mortar and pestle or spice grinder.

Put the pea crumble into a big mixing bowl and add the ground coriander, chilli, garlic, ginger, spring onion, oil and lime juice. Mix well, adding the reserved cooking water to make the dip smooth, then season to taste with salt, pepper and more lime juice, if you like. Scatter with coriander leaves and spring onions and serve.

SPLIT PEA PATTIES

Dried peas are an amazing product and we don't eat enough of them. Instead, we feed them to pigs… and then eat the pigs! We should start eating the peas themselves. They work well here as patties, or in my Nordic Guacamole (see page 60), in soup and in stews, of course, or just boiled and added to a salad.

Instead of split green peas, you can use green lentils, yellow split peas or chickpeas.

SERVES 4

For the peperonata
4 red (bell) peppers, deseeded and cut into strips
1 small garlic clove, grated (shredded)
1 tsp cumin seeds
½ tsp chilli flakes (red pepper flakes)
1 tbsp olive oil
4 tbsp chopped parsley leaves
juice of ½ lemon
sea salt flakes (kosher salt) and freshly ground
  black pepper

For the patties
150g (5½oz) green split peas
200g (7oz) courgette (zucchini)
1 medium onion, chopped
3 tbsp chopped dill
3 eggs, lightly beaten
3 tbsp plain (all-purpose) flour
2 tbsp rolled oats
½ tsp freshly grated nutmeg
1 tsp baking powder
2–3 tbsp vegetable oil
2 tbsp salted butter

Preheat the oven to 180°C/350°F/Gas Mark 4.

Place the pepper strips in an ovenproof dish, then mix in the garlic, cumin, chilli flakes and olive oil and sprinkle with salt and pepper. Bake for 30 minutes, then allow them to cool.

Put the cooled peppers in a blender and add the parsley and lemon juice, then whizz to a purée. Season with salt and pepper to taste.

Now for the patties. Cook the split peas for 30 minutes in plenty of boiling water, then drain and allow to cool.

Put the cold peas in a mixing bowl, grate (shred) in the courgette and add the onion and dill. Fold in the eggs, then the flour, oats, nutmeg and baking powder, then season to taste with salt and pepper.

Heat the oil and butter in a frying pan. Form the pea mixture into round balls, place in the pan and give them a gentle push to flatten. Fry them on both sides over a medium heat for about 10 minutes, until golden brown outside and cooked within.

Serve with the peperonata, and perhaps a nice green salad (see page 74).

TRINE'S BURNING LOVE

It may be an odd name for a dish, but this is nevertheless a famous Danish classic, classically of bacon and onion served on top of mashed potato. I am not a big bacon fan, so for years I've made a lot of other versions. Here is my take on burning love with cavolo nero.

SERVES 4–6

800g (1lb 12oz) potatoes
400g (14oz) celeriac (celery root)
2 bay leaves
65g (½ stick) salted butter, or 5 tbsp olive oil, or a mix
sea salt flakes (kosher salt) and freshly ground black pepper

For the topping
200g (7oz) beetroots (beets)
200g (7oz) cavolo nero
50g (1¾oz) walnuts
3 tbsp olive oil
2 garlic cloves, finely chopped
1 medium onion, finely chopped
Sweet and Sour Cucumber Salad, to serve (see page 35)

Peel the potatoes and celeriac, if you like, or just scrub them well; I think the skins are great in a mash and add to the flavour. Cut into big chunks, place in a saucepan, cover with water and drop in the bay leaves. Don't add salt, because it makes the mash sticky. Boil until tender, then drain (reserving the cooking water) and remove the bay leaves. Add the butter or oil, or both, with 350ml (12fl oz) of the reserved cooking water, then season well. Mash the vegetables, then whisk them with a balloon whisk to make them lighter and smoother.

Meanwhile, peel the beetroots and chop them into very small cubes, then tear the cavolo nero leaves into pieces, discarding the coarse ribs.

Tip the walnuts into a large dry frying pan (skillet) and roast them a little. When they start to brown, add the olive oil, garlic, onion and beetroots and sauté for 5 minutes. Now add the cavolo nero and sauté for a further 3–4 minutes. Season to taste with salt and pepper.

Serve the mash with the vegetable and walnut topping, with the cucumber salad on the side.

WHITE BEAN AND TOMATO TOASTS WITH POACHED EGGS

This is quite pointedly not the ubiquitous avocado toast, but it makes a fabulous snack. I think we need to start talking about why all the trendy cafés throughout Europe and America need avocado toast on their menu! It is not sustainable: avocado farming uses a lot of water and they are often transported over long distances. Avocado should be a luxury food, not an everyday affair.

SERVES 4

1 tsp coriander seeds
500g (1lb 2oz) cooked white beans
2 spring onions (scallions), sliced
1 small garlic clove, finely chopped
1 small red chilli, finely sliced
juice of ¼ lime
2 tbsp extra virgin olive oil
2 tomatoes, roughly chopped
4 slices of sourdough bread
1 tsp 5 per cent acid distilled vinegar,
    or white wine vinegar
4 eggs
sea salt flakes (kosher salt) and freshly ground
    black pepper
coriander leaves (cilantro), to serve (optional)

Toast the coriander seeds in a dry frying pan (skillet) over a medium heat for a few minutes, then grind them in a mortar and pestle or with a spice grinder.

Place the ground coriander, beans, spring onions, garlic, chilli, lime juice, olive oil and some salt and pepper in a food processor and pulse to combine. It shouldn't become a paste; it should still be rustic. Scrape into a mixing bowl and add the tomatoes, seasoning to taste with salt and pepper.

Toast the slices of sourdough bread.

Bring a saucepan of water to a steady simmer, then add the vinegar to the pan. Crack the eggs individually into small cups.

Create a gentle whirlpool in the water with a whisk, which will help each egg white to wrap around its yolk. Slowly tip two of the eggs, one at a time, into the simmering water whirlpool. Leave to cook for 3 minutes. Remove with a slotted spoon and drain on a sheet of kitchen paper (paper towel). Repeat to cook the remaining 2 eggs.

Spread the bean mix on each piece of toast and top with a poached egg. Sprinkle with pepper and coriander leaves, if you like, and serve immediately.

BAKED BLUE POTATOES WITH GOAT'S CHEESE CREAM

Potatoes come in so many varieties and are both very nutritious and climate friendly, so they ought to be part of the staple diet in northern Europe. I like to serve these as a main dish. I mean, why not? A meal can be so many different things, as world cuisine has showed us. Meat-potatoes-and-veg is not a law. Why not shift side dishes to a meal's centre and eat them with other tasty vegetables?

I serve this with a nice cabbage salad (see pages 98 and 101).

SERVES 4

1kg (2lb 4oz) blue potatoes, or regular potatoes
100g (1 stick) salted butter
1 tsp freshly grated nutmeg
6 thyme sprigs, leaves stripped, plus thyme
  flowers (optional)
sea salt flakes (kosher salt) and freshly ground
  black pepper

For the cream
150g (5½oz) creamy goat's cheese
2 tbsp full-fat Greek yogurt

Preheat the oven to 180°C/350°F/Gas Mark 4.

Scrub the potatoes, keeping the skins on, cut in half and place in an ovenproof dish. Melt the butter in a small saucepan and add salt, pepper and the nutmeg. Pour the melted butter over the potatoes. Sprinkle with the thyme, saving a little for serving. Bake in the oven for 45 minutes.

While the potatoes are in the oven, make the goat's cheese cream. Beat the goat's cheese well in a small mixing bowl, mix it with the Greek yogurt, then season to taste with salt and pepper.

When the potatoes come out of the oven, place small dots of the goat's cheese cream on top and sprinkle with the reserved thyme, or some thyme flowers, if you have those. Serve right away.

LANDGANGSBRØD, SCANDINAVIAN BRUSCHETTA

Landgangsbrød was a trend in Denmark in the 1980s. A *landgang* is a bridge that connects a ship to its mooring in a harbour. The bread used to come with a combination of toppings inspired by the *smørrebrød*, so you would have three or four different toppings – fish, meat and cheese – on the same open sandwich.

Here I have simplified that idea and made a summer treat with tomatoes when they are tasty, ripe and juicy. You can swap the feta for goat's cheese or Parmesan, depending on what you prefer and have available. I'm not sure if this is a recipe, so I hesitated to put it in the book, but the simple things really are the best!

SERVES 4

2 baguettes
2 tbsp salted butter
8 medium-sized tomatoes, ideally in
    different colours
150g (5½oz) feta cheese
6 dill sprigs
sea salt flakes (kosher salt) and freshly ground
    black pepper

Cut the baguettes lengthways, then butter each piece.

Cut the tomatoes into slices and place on top, crumble the feta and sprinkle it over the tomatoes, then sprinkle with salt and pepper.

Decorate with dill and serve right away.

SALAD AS MY MEAL

The seasons play a pivotal role in the way I cook and eat. In summer, lettuces are abundant, and because they are in season they are crisp and tasty and wonderful with a nice sharp dressing that gives them character. I love a big green salad. Give me some bread and maybe goat's cheese too – or slices of fresh tomatoes, herbs and nuts – and I'll be happy to eat just that as my summer supper. I even like the green tomatoes that haven't fully ripened late in the summer; they are tangy but still offer a little sweetness. Just a few simple elements, when combined with consideration and dressed with care, can be very satisfying.

Salads can be simple and clean in flavour, which is often how I prefer them in the summer when produce is fresh and shouts with energy. In winter, I turn to ingredients that make salads more bold and complex; warm flavours with hygge and comfort.

Although it may not be immediately obvious, biodiversity makes a huge difference to our cooking; it gives us a range of produce, which means more to work with, different varieties of apples – not just the ubiquitous Pink Lady – heritage tomatoes and radishes, unusual cabbages and so on.

To cut to the chase: fertile soil growing a range of grains and vegetables is more resilient to nature's shifting moods and whims than miles and miles of monocultural fields. Working with nature, instead of trying to fight and control it, protects the climate, makes animals want to live there, gives us cleaner food and protects our drinking water. Therefore, biodiversity on our plates is important to us all. The way to achieve it is to follow the seasons when you shop, to buy as many different varieties of vegetables as possible and to eat more vegetables than anything else. Support your local farmers' markets, or buy directly from farms, or consider enrolling in a veg box scheme.

I want my salad to be a testament to the local vegetables that are in season, mixed with spices, oils and condiments from around the world. In the summer I eat lettuces and tomatoes, in autumn I mix apples and pears into my salads, then comes winter and it's time for cabbages, citrus fruits and baked root vegetables. Suddenly – at the end of a long winter when I can't look at another carrot – spring arrives and I can finally eat asparagus and sweet green peas once more. Making salads, year after year, in a beautiful circle.

MY DAILY SALAD, WITH MY DAILY SALAD DRESSING

I think a salad for dinner is essential, and often, for me, salad is dinner, in combination with seasonal vegetables. A tasty dressing is a vital part of any salad and it can be so many different things, from just a simple mix of oil and vinegar, to versions including ginger, honey, spices, herbs or dairy. The combinations are truly endless.

This is my own classic dressing and I like to make a big portion of it so I can easily dress our daily salad. And it is endlessly versatile: often, for an easy quick dinner, I'll mix leftover potatoes, lentils or even fish with a lot of cabbage and some cucumber and then add my dressing.

SERVES 4

For the salad
350g (7oz) crisp green salad leaves
leaves from a large bunch of flat-leaf parsley
3–4 tbsp my daily salad dressing, or any other
    salad dressing you prefer

For my daily salad dressing
Makes enough for a week or two
(about 500ml/2 cups)

50ml (¼ cup) tarragon white wine vinegar
2 garlic cloves, finely grated (shredded)
2 tbsp lemon juice
3 tbsp Dijon mustard
2 tbsp honey
100ml (scant ½ cup) olive oil
250ml (1 cup) grapeseed oil
3 tbsp cold water
sea salt flakes (kosher salt) and freshly ground
    black pepper

Rinse all the salad leaves and parsley, then drain well and use a salad spinner if you have one to get them good and dry.

Place the leaves in a large mixing bowl: salad bowls must be big so there is room to toss the salad thoroughly, otherwise the dressing does not get mixed in as well as it ought to.

Toss with the dressing and serve right away.

To make my daily salad dressing:
If you have a food processor, add the vinegar, garlic, lemon juice, mustard and honey and pulse, adding both oils gradually until you have a smooth dressing, then blend in the water and season to taste.

If you are making the dressing by hand, whisk the vinegar, garlic, lemon juice, mustard and honey until you have a smooth base, then gradually whisk in the oils until you have used them all, then whisk in the water and season to taste.

Place in a glass bottle with an airtight lid and leave in the refrigerator for your daily salads.

TOMATO AND COURGETTE SALAD

Over the last decade, knowledge about different tomato varieties has grown and so many more are now available. I can think of few other vegetables that are used in so many ways. The classic Scandinavian way, *smørrebrød*, is, in the summer, a piece of rye bread, butter, tomato slices, mayo and chives: so simple, yet so tasty. I've given another variation elsewhere in this book (see page 71). I remember, as a young woman, tasting tomato and mozzarella salad with basil for the first time… I was blown away. From then on, endless tomato salad combinations were born. This goes especially well with Smoked Mackerel with Cauliflower Two Ways (see page 116).

SERVES 4

2 courgettes (zucchini), cut into 1cm (½in) slices on an angle
1 tbsp olive oil
8 tomatoes, ideally multi-coloured, sliced
50g (1¾oz) walnuts
50g (1¾oz) dill, coarse stalks removed
sea salt flakes (kosher salt) and freshly ground black pepper

For the dressing
½ garlic clove, finely grated (shredded)
½ tsp ground coriander seeds
juice of 1 lime
1 tsp granulated sugar
1 tsp freshly ground black pepper
3 tbsp vegetable oil

In a frying pan (skillet), fry the courgette slices in the olive oil on both sides, sprinkling with salt and pepper.

Place the sliced tomatoes on a platter with the courgettes.

For the dressing, in a bowl, mix together the garlic, coriander, lime juice and sugar with the pepper, then gradually whisk in the oil. Pour the dressing over the tomatoes.

Finely chop the walnuts and dill and sprinkle them evenly over the tomatoes and courgettes. Serve right away.

SPICED ROAST
NEW POTATO SALAD

There is something about potato salad that is so old school; in fact, today it seems to have almost disappeared. It is a dish from another era, one in which women danced around in long Mary Quant dresses adorned with big patterns, a glass of Dubonnet in their hand, and produced plates of cold cured meat with potato salad and a baguette as a cutting-edge dinner. I still love a good potato salad, and now, when we must cut down on meat and fish, I think it makes an excellent main course when paired with a crisp green salad. It is a very sustainable vegetable, has great nutritional value, tastes wonderful and can be used in so many ways.

SERVES 4

800g (1lb 12oz) new potatoes (fingerlings), well scrubbed
4 tbsp olive oil
1 tsp ground cumin
1 celery stick, with leaves
10 radishes
2 spring onions (scallions)
2 tbsp salted capers, rinsed and drained
juice of 1 lemon, plus more to taste
sea salt flakes (kosher salt) and freshly ground black pepper

Preheat the oven to 200°C/400°F/Gas Mark 6.

Halve the potatoes and place in an ovenproof dish, then mix in the olive oil, cumin and some salt and pepper and bake for 30 minutes.

Meanwhile, slice the celery stick and chop the leaves, chop the radishes and cut the spring onions into fine slices. Place the celery, radishes and spring onions in a mixing bowl, add the capers, mix, then season to taste with salt and pepper.

When the potatoes are done, take them out of the oven, squeeze the lemon juice over them and let rest for 15 minutes.

Gently mix the potatoes with the vegetable mixture and season to taste with salt, pepper and lemon juice. Serve right away.

Salad as my Meal

CAULIFLOWER AND SAVOY SALAD WITH FETA

Savoy cabbage has lovely crinkled leaves, is dark green on the outside, and, as you go through the tight layers within, it becomes a lighter green. The leaves are crunchy yet tender and are great raw, just finely sliced, so it feels crisp and light to eat.

SERVES 6–8, *or 4 people for 2 days*

½ Savoy cabbage (about 500g/1lb 2oz)
1 tsp sea salt flakes (kosher salt)
1 head of cauliflower (600–700g/1lb 5oz–1lb 9oz)
200g (7oz) feta cheese, crumbled
2 tbsp finely chopped preserved lemon zest, or the finely grated (shredded) zest of 1–2 lemons
leaves from a large bunch of flat-leaf parsley, chopped

For the dressing
1 small garlic clove, finely grated (shredded)
juice of 1 lime
1 tsp white wine vinegar
4 tbsp extra virgin olive oil
freshly ground black pepper

Cut the Savoy into 4 wedges and then into very fine slices. Place in a mixing bowl, massage the shreds with the sea salt flakes – this tenderizes it – and leave to rest.

Cut the cauliflower into 4 big wedges, rinse well, then drain. Now cut into fine slices from top to bottom, so the slices look like little trees. Put them in a separate bowl and mix with the feta, preserved lemon and parsley.

For the dressing, in a small bowl, whisk the garlic, lime juice and vinegar, then gradually whisk in the olive oil, seasoning to taste with salt and pepper. Now mix the Savoy cabbage with the cauliflower mixture and the dressing, toss well and season to taste once more. Serve.

HOT SMOKED SALMON, SPINACH AND FENNEL SALAD

Salmon is the fish most people link to Scandinavian food, and that is of course true, though probably more so in Norway than in Denmark. Salmon used to be connected to fine dining or special occasions; today it is the most eaten fish at home in Denmark. It is not cheap, but it is very easy to cook. Both cold- and hot-smoked salmon are great to have on hand for simple, quick meals.

SERVES 4

100g (3½oz) spinach
1 fennel bulb, about 150g (5½oz)
400g (14oz) hot-smoked salmon, skinned
½ lemon

For the dressing
100g (scant ½ cup) natural yogurt
4 tbsp lemon juice
½ tsp chilli flakes (red pepper flakes)
sea salt flakes (kosher salt) and freshly ground
   black pepper

Wash the spinach very well; you may need several changes of water to get the leaves properly clean. Cut the fennel into super-fine slices, using a mandoline if you have one. If you want them to curl, place them in iced water for a few minutes, before draining well and drying. Flake the salmon into large pieces.

In a small bowl, mix together all the ingredients for the dressing and season to taste with salt and pepper.

In a large bowl, mix the spinach, fennel and salmon, fold in the dressing and place in a serving bowl. Squeeze the ½ lemon over the fish, sprinkle with more black pepper and serve right away.

SUMMER CABBAGE WITH PRAWNS AND RADISHES

———————

I like to eat cabbage every day. I love the taste, the crunchy mouth-feel and the knowledge that it is healthy; I can sense my body thanking me as I eat it. However, if you're going to eat cabbage daily, you need variety, and you also need to respect the seasons. Some varieties of cabbage are available in autumn and winter, others in spring and summer. Any cabbage can be paired with endless combinations of other vegetables and dressings. A few times during summer I treat myself to prawns (shrimp); I really love prawns, but they must be fresh and caught responsibly. I boil and peel them and add them to the salad. You can also use frozen prawns, or ready-peeled prawns. When there are no prawns, I simply make the salad without them, or sometimes I add boiled potatoes.

SERVES 4

500g (1lb 2oz) raw cold-water prawns
   (small cold-water shrimp)
1 summer cabbage
1 long cucumber
10 radishes
200g (7oz) shelled fresh peas (garden peas)
large bunch of dill, coarse stalks removed,
   chopped

For the dressing
2 tsp Dijon mustard
2–3 tbsp lemon juice
1 tsp white wine vinegar
3–4 tbsp grapeseed oil
sea salt flakes (kosher salt) and freshly ground
   black pepper

Start with preparing the prawns: boil them in salted water for a few minutes, then drain and peel them and store in the refrigerator until needed.

Chop the cabbage into slices 5mm (¼in) thick, rinse in cold water and drain well.

Halve the cucumber lengthways, scrape out the seeds with a teaspoon, then cut it into half moons. Cut the radishes into fine slices: if you have a mandoline, use that.

Mix all the salad ingredients in a large mixing bowl. Make sure it is a big bowl, so there is enough room to toss the salad adequately, or it won't taste as good.

Now mix the dressing. Place the mustard, lemon juice and vinegar in a mixing bowl and whisk, then gradually whisk in the oil, seasoning to taste with salt and pepper.

Gently toss the salad with the dressing, then serve straight away.

FENNEL, TOMATO AND HERB SALAD WITH CROUTONS

There is something magical about fennel… when treated properly. That little bulb can be dull when chopped into big, ungainly chunks and not cooked with love, but, if sliced super-fine, it's great, giving texture and a light flavour that works so well with many other vegetables. I think it is an especially good match with tomatoes.

SERVES 8

1 tbsp fennel seeds
1 fennel bulb, finely sliced, with its fronds
1 cucumber, sliced into chunks
400g (14oz) tomatoes, cut into wedges
   (a mix of colours is nice)
2 tbsp salted capers, rinsed and drained
leaves from a bunch of flat-leaf parsley, chopped
10 mint leaves, chopped
Croutons (see page 23)

For the dressing
1 tbsp white wine vinegar
1 tsp honey
2 tbsp extra virgin olive oil
sea salt flakes (kosher salt) and freshly ground
   black pepper

Roast the fennel seeds in a dry frying pan (skillet) until light brown, then tip out on to a plate and allow to cool.

Whisk the vinegar and honey for the dressing in a small bowl, then gradually whisk in the oil. Season to taste with salt and pepper.

Mix the vegetables, capers, herbs, roasted fennel seeds and croutons, pour over the dressing, toss gently and serve right away.

PEACH, BRIE AND BALSAMIC ALMOND SALAD

I adore ripe, juicy peaches, especially when eaten on a hot, sunny day. Peaches from Southern Europe have always been part of the Danish summer, but they do not always reach us ripe and juicy. I buy them anyway, in the hope that they will be perfect (though that happens rarely). Frying them in butter brings their sweetness out, so, when the fruit is a little disappointing, I make this salad.

SERVES 4

40g (1½oz) almonds
2 tsp honey
1 tbsp balsamic vinegar
100g (3½oz) rocket (arugula), mizuna or other mixed leaves
1 creamy ripe Brie
4 peaches
1 tbsp salted butter
sea salt flakes (kosher salt) and freshly ground black pepper
edible wild flowers, to serve (optional)

For the dressing
1 tsp honey
1 tbsp balsamic vinegar
2 tbsp extra virgin olive oil

Line a baking tray with baking parchment. Toast the almonds in a dry frying pan (skillet) until they are light brown. Add the honey and stir well, then add the balsamic and let simmer for a few minutes. Tip the almonds out of the pan on to the prepared tray and leave to cool. Do not touch them: they will be very hot, like caramel.

Place the salad leaves in a serving bowl. Cut the Brie into small pieces.

Stone the peaches and cut them into wedges. Fry on all sides in a frying pan in the butter until golden brown, sprinkling with plenty of black pepper. Then arrange them on the salad leaves with the Brie.

With wet hands, take the cooled almonds off the baking parchment; the cold water on your hands makes this easier. Chop on a chopping board and scatter them over the peaches and Brie.

Whisk the honey and balsamic vinegar for the dressing in a small bowl, then gradually whisk in the oil.

Drizzle the dressing over the salad, then decorate with flower petals, if using. Serve right away.

HERITAGE BEAN SALAD

Every spring I get multi-coloured beans from Stensbølgård, the local farm that I have worked with for many years. From spring to winter they produce the most flavour-filled vegetables I have ever eaten. I just love to cook with such fresh ingredients, nothing compares to it. Each year I get so excited when the beans arrive. They are in season for just two or three weeks, during which I make a series of bean salads, stews and even mix them with eggs for breakfast.

SERVES 4

600g (1lb 5oz) multi-coloured string beans,
   or you can use regular green beans
2 tbsp olive oil
1 red onion, sliced
1 tbsp coriander seeds
150g (5½oz) cherry tomatoes
4 tbsp finely chopped parsley leaves
juice of 1 lemon
sea salt flakes (kosher salt) and freshly ground
   black pepper

Rinse the beans and remove the stalk ends.

Put the olive oil in a frying pan, add the red onion and coriander seeds and sauté for 3–4 minutes, then add the beans and sauté for another 5 minutes.

Meanwhile, cut the tomatoes in half.

Turn the heat off under the frying pan and add the tomatoes, parsley and lemon juice. Mix well and season to taste with salt and pepper. Let it rest for 10 minutes before serving.

Salad as my Meal

CHERRY AND
SPINACH SALAD

A summer treat, to which you can successfully add Parmesan or blue cheese. I serve this with meatballs, smoked or pan-fried mackerel, beetroot patties and so much more.

SERVES 4

50g (1¾oz) almonds
1 tbsp honey
4 tbsp balsamic vinegar
150g (5½oz) spinach leaves
500g (1lb 2oz) cherries
2 tbsp olive oil
sea salt flakes (kosher salt) and freshly ground
    black pepper

Have a sheet of baking parchment to hand.

Line a baking tray with baking parchment. Toast the almonds in a dry frying pan (skillet) until they are light brown. Add the honey and stir well, then add 2 tablespoons of the balsamic and let it simmer for a few minutes. Tip the almonds out of the pan on to the prepared tray and leave to cool. Do not touch them: they will be very hot, like caramel. When the nuts have cooled, chop them.

Rinse the spinach in water (you may need to do this several times to get it properly clean), then drain well and place it on a dish. In a frying pan, fry the cherries (with their stems intact) in the oil for about 5 minutes over a medium heat, then add the remaining 2 tbsp balsamic vinegar, toss the cherries in the pan and let them simmer for a final 2 minutes. Turn off the heat and let the cherries cool in the pan.

When the cherries have cooled, spread them over the spinach, making sure all the dressing in the pan is drizzled over as well. Sprinkle the almonds on top, season with salt and pepper, then serve.

SWEET GREEN
TOMATO SALAD

I am not sure if I ever ate green tomatoes before I watched the movie *Fried Green Tomatoes*, though I knew unripe tomatoes were used in pickles, so as not to go to waste. Now there are sweet, fully ripe green varieties available in the summer, though their season is short. They are juicy, with the slight taste of garden peas. A green tomato salad is beautiful, so enchanting, though of course this recipe can also be made with red or yellow tomatoes. Here I combine them with asparagus and toasted coriander seeds.

SERVES 4

2 tbsp coriander seeds
3 tbsp grapeseed oil, or sunflower oil
6 large green tomatoes
10 violet or green asparagus spears
juice of 1 lime
2 tbsp chive flowers, or other edible flowers
4 tbsp chopped dill
4 tbsp chopped coriander (cilantro)
sea salt flakes (kosher salt) and freshly ground
    black pepper

Toast the coriander seeds in a frying pan (skillet) with the oil until they are light brown and begin to pop. Turn off the heat and leave in the pan until cool.

Slice the tomatoes thickly and place on a platter. Snap off the lowest one-third of the asparagus spears and discard (or save for a stock or soup, see page 59). Cut the raw asparagus into fine slices on an angle. Spread the asparagus evenly over the tomatoes.

Sprinkle over the coriander seeds and their oil, then drizzle over the lime juice.

Scatter the flowers and herbs over the salad, sprinkle with salt and pepper and serve right away.

Salad as my Meal

BLACK AND WHITE SALAD

I always cook fresh rice for a salad. Cold rice from the refrigerator is often floury and not that tasty (when I have leftover cooked rice, I prefer to fry it). Beluga lentils are very delicious, flaky and firm. I always feel great when I eat this salad; I find both the flavour and the texture truly comforting.

SERVES 4

150g (5½oz) beluga lentils
150g (5½oz) white basmati rice
10 asparagus spears, trimmed and cut into
   5mm (¼in) slices
1 celery stick, chopped into 5mm (¼in) slices
large bunch of dill, coarse stalks removed,
   chopped

For the dressing
juice of 1 lemon
1 tbsp white wine vinegar
4 tbsp extra virgin olive oil
sea salt flakes (kosher salt) and freshly ground
   black pepper

Boil the beluga lentils in plenty of water for 30 minutes, then drain and allow to cool.

Bring the rice to the boil in 500ml (2 cups) water in a saucepan, then reduce the heat and let it simmer for 10 minutes. Cover and let it rest under the lid for 10 minutes, then allow to cool.

For the dressing, whisk the lemon juice and vinegar, then gradually whisk in the oil and season well.

Put the cooled lentils and rice in a large mixing bowl and gently mix in the vegetables and dill. Toss gently with the dressing and mix into the salad, seasoning to taste.

RED CABBAGE, PEAR AND WALNUT SALAD

This is so simple and is my go-to winter salad. I serve it with Celeriac-Potato Patties with Parsley Pesto (see page 53) as a main meal, or, for lunch, with a slice of toasted rye bread and some soft goat's cheese. If you do not have pears, you can use apples instead. If you have any kale, you can also add that, as this recipe can be made with a mix of cabbage. This is also amazing for Christmas, as it goes well with turkey or duck.

SERVES 4

1 tbsp grapeseed oil, or sunflower oil
2 red onions, cut into wedges
1 small red cabbage
2 pears
75g (2¾oz) walnuts
sea salt flakes (kosher salt) and freshly ground
   black pepper

For the dressing
1 tbsp Dijon mustard
1 tsp honey
1 tbsp white wine vinegar
3 tbsp grapeseed oil, or sunflower oil

Put the oil into a frying pan, add the onions and gently sauté until they are cooked but still crisp, then sprinkle with salt and pepper.

Cut the red cabbage in 5mm (¼in) slices and finely slice the pears. Fry them both in a dry pan for few minutes. Chop the walnuts roughly.

Mix all the salad ingredients together in a mixing bowl.

For the dressing, whisk the mustard, honey and vinegar together. Now drizzle in the oil and season with salt and pepper.

Fold the dressing into the cabbage salad and season to taste with salt and pepper.

Salad as my Meal

WINTER CABBAGE SALAD WITH POMEGRANATE

Aren't we lucky to be living at a time where there seems to be no end to the different ways in which brassicas can be cooked? New methods seem to emerge every week from the kitchens of the world's most cutting-edge restaurants. For generations before us, brassicas were only served well cooked, sweet and sour, or salted. All perfectly good ways to serve them, of course, but there is so much more to them, as we are discovering today.

SERVES 4

150g (5½oz) Brussels sprouts, trimmed
150g (5½oz) kale, coarse stalks removed
50g (1¾oz) almonds, skin on
2 blood oranges
seeds of 1 pomegranate

For the dressing
2 tbsp lime juice
juice of 1 pomegranate
1 tsp honey
3 tbsp grapeseed oil
sea salt flakes (kosher salt) and freshly ground
    black pepper

Cut the Brussels sprouts into slices, chop the kale roughly and mix both in a large bowl.

Toast the almonds in a dry frying pan (skillet), then chop them.

Cut the peel off the blood oranges, then cut the fruit into slices.

Now in a mixing bowl, mix all the greens, almonds and fruit.

For the dressing, whisk the lime juice, pomegranate juice and honey, then gradually whisk in the oil. Gently mix into the salad. Season to taste with salt and pepper and serve right away.

Salad as my Meal

LIGHT
DINNERS

For a lot of people, everyday cooking can pose such a challenge that they often choose takeaways or ready meals instead. I don't think I can change that, but if you are one of those people and I can inspire you to cook just three or four times a week, it would mean the world to me.

The problem with ready meals is that there is often too much salt in them and not enough vegetables, unless you buy salads, then I am picky about the dressing, and so it goes on and on…

Of course, it is easy for me to turn my back on ready meals and takeaways. I am a cook, so creating meals happens as part of the ebb and flow of my working life. I can shop once a week, making sure I maximize the potential of my refrigerator and cupboard. Then when I come home at night, I decide what to cook and whether I want to spend a long or short time over it. For me, cooking in my kitchen is relaxing, I am in my element. I have a vast array of spices, vinegars, oils, sauces and all kinds of homemade nerdy stuff at my fingertips… all of this because I am a cook.

I know that most people don't start from my lucky position when it comes to deciding what to make for dinner. However, tasty healthy homemade meals are possible for everyone. There are a few small changes that will help. Be sure to have a nice selection of spices, at least one good olive oil, a neutral-tasting oil, soy sauce and a few vinegars: white wine, apple cider and balsamic. Get in a few different types of nuts, some sesame seeds and mustard. Then you will be off to a good start. The other secret is to plan, sit down with a cup of tea and spend a little time thinking about what you will need to buy for meals to eat over the next three or four days. Cook double portions, so you have enough for two days running, or to stash some in the freezer. Nothing tastes better than leftovers.

Keep crusts of bread: stale bread makes good croutons. Save the ends of the vegetables: the one-third of a cabbage, the single onion or carrot, even if they seem floppy and past it. They will all turn into a nice velvety, creamy soup at the end of the week. For this, of course, you will have to invest in a blender or hand blender. But it won't be a sunk cost: it will mean no more of the food you have bought will be wasted.

What I am advocating here is this: try to cook at least some days during the week. It's good for your budget, for the planet and for your health and general wellbeing. It will lighten the load all around.

The vegetable-centred, easy-to-digest recipes in this chapter make this way of no-waste cooking relaxing, tasty and nourishing for you and your family every day.

FRITTATA WITH ASPARAGUS

For me, this works for both breakfast or dinner. I know I write it a lot, but understanding and respecting the seasons is key to improving our climate, so let's eat vegetables only when they are in season. I eat asparagus several times a week when it is in season. I prefer, though, to buy only hyper-local asparagus, if possible. Check your farmers' market wherever you live, buy what they have on offer and plan your cooking that way.

If you can find wild asparagus, then you can also use that in this dish.

SERVES 4

20 slim asparagus spears
8 eggs
3 tbsp finely grated (shredded) Parmesan cheese
1 tbsp olive oil
10 spring onions (scallions), sliced lengthways
sea salt flakes (kosher salt) and freshly ground
  black pepper
fresh herbs and edible flowers (optional), to serve

Break the woody ends off the asparagus spears where they snap (you can use these for soup, see page 59), then cut each spear in half lengthways.

Lightly beat the eggs in a bowl and add the Parmesan with some salt and pepper.

Heat the olive oil in a large frying pan (skillet) and sauté the spring onions for 5 minutes, then add the asparagus and sauté for a further few minutes, sprinkling with salt and pepper.

Add the egg mixture to the frying pan and gently fold into the vegetables with a wooden spoon until the eggs have lightly set but are still creamy.

Serve, decorated with herbs and flowers, if you like.

SPRING *FRIKASSÉ*

─────────────

A Danish classic originally made with braised veal, though I have come to prefer this vegetable version. When spring arrives, this is the first dish I think of cooking, to celebrate the lighter days ahead.

SERVES 4

15–20 asparagus spears
2 garlic cloves, chopped
2 tbsp salted butter
600g (1lb 5oz) small new potatoes (fingerlings),
    well-scrubbed and halved
200ml (generous ¾ cup) white wine
1 bay leaf
5 thyme sprigs
6 spring onions (scallions), cut into 3cm
    (1¼in) pieces
200g (7oz) radishes, halved
200ml (generous ¾ cup) double (heavy) cream
200g (7oz) shelled fresh peas (garden peas)
½ tsp freshly grated nutmeg
2 chervil sprigs, chopped
sea salt flakes (kosher salt) and freshly ground
    black pepper

Break the woody ends off the asparagus spears where they snap (you can use these for soup, see page 59), then cut each spear into 3 pieces.

In a sauté pan for which you have a lid, sauté the garlic in the butter over a medium heat for a few minutes. Add the potatoes, wine, bay leaf and thyme, season with salt, cover and let it simmer until the potatoes are al dente. This should take 7–10 minutes; check with the tip of a knife.

Now add the spring onions, radishes, asparagus and cream, bring to the boil, then reduce the heat and allow to simmer for 3–4 minutes. Add the peas and allow to warm through, then season with the nutmeg and some salt and pepper and scatter over the chervil.

Serve straight away, in warmed dishes.

ROAST TOMATO SOUP

A super-easy way to make a tasty soup in the oven in 30 minutes, to be served hot or cold.
I always, actually, eat this when I'm at the beach, which is an everyday event here in Denmark
since sandy beaches run along most of the coastline. So, you could say this is my summer tomato
soup. However, you never know what the weather is going to be like, so here is a cold soup for
sunny days, or a hot soup for when it rains!

SERVES 4

1.5kg (3lb 5oz) plum tomatoes, ideally
  San Marzano
2 onions, chopped
2 garlic cloves, chopped
4 tbsp olive oil
1 tbsp coriander seeds
leaves from a small bunch of basil
200ml (generous ¾ cup) water
sea salt flakes (kosher salt) and freshly ground
  black pepper

To serve (optional)
Croutons (optional, see page 23), or bread
full-fat crème fraîche
spring onions (scallions), or chives, or chive
  flowers, finely chopped

Preheat the oven to 200°C/400°F/Gas Mark 6.
Line a baking tray with baking parchment.

Cut the tomatoes in half and place with the
onions and garlic on the prepared baking tray.
Drizzle the olive oil over the tomatoes and
sprinkle with the coriander seeds and some
salt and pepper. Roast for 30 minutes.

Take the baking tray out of the oven and place
the contents in a blender with the basil. Blitz
into a soup; it should be a bit lumpy. Place
in a saucepan with the water and bring to the
boil, then season to taste.

Serve right away with croutons or bread, crème
fraîche and spring onions or chives or chive
flowers, or cool down and chill, to serve cold.

CHICORY, SALMON AND BLOOD ORANGE SALAD

Bitter chicory, sweet smoked salmon and acidic blood oranges are just an amazing match. This is a salad I like to serve in the winter months; it is especially fitting and festive at Christmas time.

SERVES 4

4 heads of chicory
2 tbsp olive oil
4 blood oranges
8 large slices of smoked salmon
juice of ½ lemon
3–4 large radicchio leaves
3 dill sprigs
sea salt flakes (kosher salt) and freshly ground
   black pepper
baguette, or another delicious bread, to serve

Cut each chicory head into 4 long wedges lengthways. Heat the olive oil in a frying pan (skillet) and fry the chicory on each side, sprinkling with salt and pepper. When done, place in 4 serving bowls.

Cut the peel from the blood oranges, then slice the fruit and arrange it in between the chicory wedges on the plates. Place the salmon slices in the salad and squeeze the lemon juice over them. Chop the radicchio into fine slices, chop the dill and sprinkle both over the salad.

Season with black pepper and serve with crusty bread.

CHILLED PEA POD SOUP

———————————————

Whenever I can get hold of fresh peas (garden peas), I like to make this soup. If the peas are organic and fresh, you can use their pods instead of the sugarsnaps here; they give an amazing texture and flavour. In winter, you can use frozen peas and serve the soup warm with a dash of Greek yogurt and some chilli sauce.

SERVES 4

500g (1lb 2oz) fresh peas (garden peas), weighed without pods; reserve the pods
2 tbsp olive oil
1 tsp salted butter
2 shallots, finely chopped
200g (7oz) sugarsnaps (optional)
1 litre (1 quart) vegetable stock
¼ nutmeg, freshly grated
3–4 tbsp lemon juice
sea salt flakes (kosher salt) and freshly ground black pepper

To serve
Croutons (see page 23)
chervil leaves, or parsley leaves

Start by shelling the peas. If they are organic and very fresh, you can also use the pods, though you will need to remove the strings down both sides.

Heat the oil and butter in a sauté pan and cook the shallots until they are translucent. Now either add the sugarsnaps or pea pods, whichever you are using, mix well, then pour in the stock. Bring to the boil and allow to boil for 3 minutes, then add the shelled peas, return to the boil, then turn the heat off.

Blitz the soup in a blender or food processor; the texture should be rustic, not too smooth. Season with the nutmeg, lemon juice and some salt and pepper. Leave to cool, then chill in the refrigerator.

Serve the chilled soup scattered with croutons and chervil or parsley leaves.

SPINACH PATTIES WITH TOMATO AND LIME SALSA

A vegetarian alternative to the traditional Danish meatballs. I have been eating these tasty little *spinachdeller* since I was a little girl.

SERVES 4

300g (10½oz) white bread, weighed without crust
1 onion, chopped
2 tbsp salted butter, plus more to fry the patties
200ml (generous ¾ cup) single (light) cream
600g (1lb 5oz) spinach, coarse stems removed
3 eggs, lightly beaten
½ tsp freshly grated nutmeg, or to taste
sea salt flakes (kosher salt) and freshly ground
  black pepper
grapeseed oil, to fry

For the salsa
4 plum tomatoes, ideally San Marzano
juice of ½ lime
1 tbsp extra virgin olive oil
½ garlic clove, finely chopped
1 spring onion (scallion), finely chopped

Crumble the bread into a large mixing bowl. In a saucepan, sauté the onion in the 2 tbsp butter until translucent, then add the onion to the breadcrumbs with the cream. Mix well with your hands, then leave to rest for a couple of hours.

Rinse the spinach in cold water and leave to drain in a colander. Blend the drained spinach until it is finely chopped, then mix it into the bread mixture with the eggs, seasoning with the nutmeg, salt and pepper.

For the salsa, finely chop the tomatoes and mix with the lime juice, olive oil, garlic and spring onion, then season to taste with salt and pepper.

It is always a good idea to test the meatball mixture to check if it is seasoned correctly, so take a teaspoon of it and fry for a few minutes, then you can taste to see if it needs more salt, pepper or nutmeg.

Heat some butter and oil in a frying pan (skillet). Make oval balls of the mixture with a big tablespoon, giving each of them a light squeeze to firm them up. Fry for 4–5 minutes on each side, then serve with the salsa.

SMOKED MACKEREL WITH CAULIFLOWER TWO WAYS

When I was a child, smoked mackerel was always served in August when the fish grew the
biggest and therefore were more fatty. If you can't get a whole fish, fillets will also do the job.
The oily mackerel and light cauliflower are a really great match.

SERVES 4

1 cauliflower
50g (½ stick) salted butter
½ tsp freshly grated nutmeg
2 tbsp chopped dill
2 tbsp olive oil
1 onion, sliced
1 garlic clove, finely chopped
4 tomatoes, sliced into wedges
2 tbsp capers
2 tbsp sunflower oil
2 lemons
2 spring onions (scallions), sliced
1 whole smoked mackerel
sea salt flakes (kosher salt) and freshly ground
   black pepper

Rinse the cauliflower and cut it in half, then
cut each half into small florets and chop the
stalk as well.

Melt the butter in a sauté pan, add half the
cauliflower, sprinkle with salt and pepper,
cover and let it simmer in the butter for about
8 minutes or until soft. When soft, blend to
a purée and season with the nutmeg, salt and
pepper, then stir in the dill. Keep it warm.

Take the (clean) sauté pan, add the olive
oil and sauté the onion and garlic for a few
minutes, then add the remaining cauliflower
and let it simmer for 4 minutes. Add the
tomatoes and season to taste with salt and
pepper, then simmer for 5 minutes more.

In a small frying pan (skillet), fry the capers in
the sunflower oil until crisp. Drain the capers
on kitchen paper (paper towel) and discard the
oil. Cut the lemons in half and fry them, flesh
side down, in the empty frying pan until they
are light brown.

Place the cauliflower purée in a bowl and
sprinkle with the spring onion and capers.
Serve with the sautéed cauliflower, smoked
mackerel and charred lemons for squeezing.

PARSLEY, ANCHOVY AND HAZELNUT LINGUINE

As a child, I never saw my *mormor* use flat-leaf parsley, only ever the curly variety. And curly parsley is great for pasta sauce, especially when it is finely chopped, as it is a little more bitter than its flat-leafed cousin, with big, 'green' flavours.

SERVES 4

8 anchovy fillets in oil
500g (1lb 2oz) linguine
100ml (scant ½ cup) olive oil
2 garlic cloves, finely sliced
75g (2¾oz) hazelnuts, chopped
leaves from a large bunch of curly parsley (about 100g/3½oz), or flat-leaf parsley, finely chopped
2 tsp coarsely ground black pepper
sea salt flakes (kosher salt)

In a small bowl, mash the anchovies with a fork to a paste.

Bring plenty of salted water to a boil, then boil the pasta for 8–9 minutes until al dente.

Meanwhile, pour the oil into a sauté pan, add the anchovy paste and sauté for 2 minutes. Now add the garlic and hazelnuts and sauté for another 5 minutes over a medium heat; the garlic should not brown. Add 2–3 tbsp of the boiling pasta water and the parsley and let it all simmer.

Drain the pasta, reserving some of its cooking water.

Add the pasta to the parsley-hazelnut sauce, gently fold in and, if it seems dry, add a little more of the cooking water. Season to taste with salt, add the coarsely ground black pepper and serve straight away.

FISKEFRIKADELLER FISH CAKES WITH HERB YOGURT SAUCE

Fish cakes can be made in so many ways. There is an old-school variety often sold in Danish fishmongers which is really a kind of 'granny-recipe'. Some years ago, a lovely boy called Benjamin lived next door to my house; he thought his mother's cooking was a bit too modern. One day, he asked me: 'Trine, can you make real fish cakes?' He was only six years old, but I knew what he meant and what he wanted. I said: 'yes' and we agreed on a dinner date. He was sceptical, as I suspect he thought I was the same type of cook as his mother, but I cooked the fish cakes just as he wished. He was very satisfied and his opinion of me improved! This is not Benjamin's recipe, but an updated version with more flavour and texture. He would probably not approve… These are good with potatoes and cabbage on the side.

SERVES 4

600g (1lb 5oz) pollack fillet, or other firm white fish fillet
100g (3½oz) carrots, grated (shredded)
1 onion, grated (shredded)
4 tbsp finely chopped parsley leaves
2 tbsp finely chopped tarragon leaves
2 eggs, lightly beaten
100ml (scant ½ cup) single (light) cream
75g (2¾oz) small (not jumbo) rolled oats
4 tbsp plain (all-purpose) flour
100ml (scant ½ cup) sparkling water
2 tsp sea salt flakes (kosher salt)
2 tbsp salted butter
2–3 tbsp neutral-tasting vegetable oil
freshly ground black pepper
lemon slices, to serve
herb flowers, to serve (optional)

For the sauce
300g (10½oz) full-fat crème fraîche
200g (7oz) carrot, coarsely grated (shredded)
leaves from a large bunch of parsley, finely chopped
large bunch of dill, coarse stalks removed, finely chopped
finely grated (shredded) zest of 1 lemon
2–3 tbsp lemon juice

Preheat the oven to 180°C/350°F/Gas Mark 4.

Chop the fish finely with a sharp knife, or use a food processor. Place in a large mixing bowl and add the carrots, onion, herbs, eggs and cream. Now add the oats and flour and mix again; finally fold in the sparkling water and season with the salt, then pepper to taste.

Melt the butter with the oil in a large frying pan (skillet) over a medium heat. Form oval-shaped balls of the fish mix with a tablespoon, using your free hand to help. Place them gently in the melted butter mixture and fry for about 4 minutes on each side. With a slotted spoon, transfer the fish cakes to an ovenproof dish and bake them in the oven for about 10 minutes.

Meanwhile, make the sauce. In a mixing bowl, mix the crème fraîche, carrot, herbs and lemon zest, then season to taste with lemon juice, salt and pepper.

Serve the *fiskefrikadeller* with the sauce and lemon slices, and a sprinkling of herb flowers, if you like and have them to hand.

ONE-POT FISH AND VEGGIES

Fish and vegetables are perfect for a light dinner. You can use more or less whatever vegetables you've got. I always have enough mixed vegetables in my refrigerator to cook this dish, then I just need to bicycle to the fishmonger to see what is on offer and I am ready to make dinner.

SERVES 4

500g (1lb 2oz) broccoli, cut into long florets
6 spring onions (scallions), sliced
2 carrots, cut into 2–4 lengthways, depending on size
2 lemons, halved lengthways, then sliced
2 tbsp olive oil
6 thyme sprigs
600–700g (1lb 5oz–1lb 9oz) haddock fillet, or other firm white fish fillet
4 tsp salted butter
sea salt flakes (kosher salt) and freshly ground black pepper
My Daily Salad (see page 74), or another green salad, to serve

Preheat the oven to 180°C/350°F/Gas Mark 4.

Mix the broccoli, spring onions, carrots and lemons in an ovenproof dish, then add the olive oil and thyme, season with salt and pepper and toss to coat everything in the oil and flavourings. Bake in the oven for 5 minutes.

Cut the fish into 4 pieces and arrange on top of the vegetables, sprinkle with salt and pepper and place 1 tsp of the butter on each piece of fish.

Return the dish to the oven and bake for a further 5 minutes, or until the fish is done. Be careful not to overcook it: if the fish flesh separates into flakes when pushed lightly, it is ready.

Serve right away with a green salad.

ONE CHICKEN: TWO DAYS

This is a way to feed four people a main meal for two days, which is both economical and more sustainable. I start by curing the chicken lightly, as it gives a firmness to the flesh and enhances the bird's flavour. You will have to do this the day before you want to eat the first chicken recipe.

OVERNIGHT BRINED CHICKEN

MAKES 1 BRINED CHICKEN

2 litres (scant 2 quarts) water
100g (3½oz) white sugar (any sugar is fine here)
20g (¾oz) sea salt flakes (kosher salt)
5 thyme sprigs
5 bay leaves
1 large free-range chicken, 1.5–2kg
   (3lb 5oz–4lb 8oz)

The day before you want to eat the chicken, boil the water in a large saucepan with the sugar, salt, thyme and bay leaves until both the sugar and salt have dissolved. Leave to cool. Find a container that will fit both the chicken and the brine and which will fit into your refrigerator. When the brine is fully cool, place the chicken in the brine. Make sure all the chicken is under the brine and that it stays under the surface (you may need to add a plate and a weight to achieve this). Leave in the refrigerator overnight.

CHICKEN IN HORSERADISH SAUCE

SERVES 4

1 Overnight Brined Chicken (see above)
2 tbsp salted butter
2 shallots, finely chopped
1 fennel bulb, chopped into slim wedges
100ml (scant ½ cup) white wine
300ml (1¼ cups) double (heavy) cream
6 tbsp grated (shredded) horseradish
200g (7oz) shelled fresh peas (garden peas)
5 dill sprigs, torn

Bring a very large saucepan of water to the boil, then reduce the heat to a gentle simmer. Take the chicken out of the brine and simmer it in the boiling water for 1 hour. Carefully remove the chicken from the liquid and place in a large, shallow dish

Take the chicken breasts off the bone, cover and set in the refrigerator for dinner tomorrow. Take the rest of the chicken meat off the carcass and chop it into smaller pieces.

Continued overleaf…

sea salt flakes (kosher salt) and freshly ground
   black pepper
boiled new potatoes (fingerlings), to serve

In a saucepan, melt the butter and sauté the
shallots, then add the fennel and pour in
the wine. Bring to the boil, then reduce the
heat and let it simmer for 5 minutes. Add the
cream and horseradish and return to the boil,
then reduce the heat and let it simmer for
another few minutes.

Add the chicken and peas and season to taste
with salt and pepper. Add the dill and serve
with boiled new potatoes.

CHICKEN AND SUMMER VEGETABLE STIR-FRY WITH HERB PESTO

This is a lovely summer dish. Serve it with bread.

SERVES 4

6 green asparagus spears
6 white asparagus spears
2 shallots, finely chopped
8 new carrots, with green tops, halved
   lengthways
1 tbsp neutral-tasting vegetable oil
2 cooked Overnight Brined Chicken breasts
   (see page 125)
large bunch of chervil, or parsley
freshly ground black pepper

For the pesto
50g (1¾oz) curly parsley
50g (1¾oz) dill
50g (1¾oz) coriander (cilantro)
40g (1½oz) almonds
1 garlic clove
100ml (scant ½ cup) extra virgin olive oil
2 tbsp lemon juice, plus more to taste
sea salt flakes (kosher salt)

For the pesto, blend all the ingredients in a
food processor into a smooth paste, seasoning
to taste with salt and maybe more lemon juice.

Snap the lower one-third off both types of
asparagus. Peel the white asparagus spears
from the tips down; when they are a little
shiny, you know you have removed enough
peel. Cut all the asparagus into 4cm (1½in)
lengths. (You can use the peels and trimmings
for soup, see page 59.)

Sauté the shallots and carrots in the oil in a
large frying pan (skillet) for a few minutes,
then add all the asparagus and sauté for a
further 2–3 minutes.

Slice the chicken breasts, add to the asparagus
and season to taste with salt and pepper. Now
mix in the chervil or parsley and serve warm,
with the pesto.

SPRINGTIME ORECCHIETTE

Springtime is green, and green is the colour of hope because – of course – it comes in exchange for the dark and cloudy winter months. I find that eating green-coloured foods really lifts my spirits in spring.

SERVES 4

500g (1lb 2oz) orecchiette pasta
15 green asparagus spears, trimmed and
    cut into 1cm (½in) pieces
1 courgette (zucchini), about 200g (7oz),
    cut into 5mm (¼in) cubes
6 tbsp extra virgin olive oil
2 garlic cloves, chopped
2 spring onions (scallions), sliced into
    1cm (½in) pieces
100g (3½oz) shelled fresh peas (garden peas)
1 tbsp finely chopped mint leaves
5 dill sprigs, finely chopped
3–4 tbsp lemon juice
sea salt flakes (kosher salt) and freshly ground
    black pepper

Bring plenty of salted water to the boil and cook the orecchiette for 8–9 minutes, or until al dente.

Snap the lower one-third of the asparagus off, then cut the spears into 1cm (½in) pieces. (The trimmings and peelings can be used in soup, see page 59.)

Meanwhile, in a sauté pan, sauté the courgette in the olive oil for 3–4 minutes. Add the garlic and spring onions and sauté for a few more minutes, then for a final minute add the asparagus, peas and herbs.

Drain the pasta, reserving some of the cooking water.

Add the pasta to the vegetable sauce, gently fold it in, and, if it seems too dry, add a little of the cooking water. Season to taste with the lemon juice, salt and pepper and serve immediately.

LEEK TART

Rye flour is sweet and earthy and it really brings out the flavour of leeks. I have never really made savoury pastry with white flour alone; a rye combination both tastes better and is crunchier once baked.

SERVES 4–6

For the pastry
125g (4½oz) plain (all-purpose) flour, plus more to dust
75g (2¾oz) stoneground wholemeal (wholegrain) rye flour
1 tsp sea salt flakes (kosher salt)
75g (½ stick plus 1 tbsp) salted butter, chopped, plus more for the dish
75g (2¾oz) full-fat skyr, quark or fromage frais

For the filling
6 leeks, cut into 2cm (¾in) slices and well washed (see page 30)
leaves from 5 thyme sprigs, chopped
2 tbsp salted butter
5 eggs
100g (3½oz) full-fat crème fraîche
200g (7oz) Comté or Cheddar cheese, grated (shredded)
1 tsp freshly grated nutmeg
freshly ground black pepper

Begin with the pastry. Mix both flours and the salt together in a large bowl, then rub in the butter with your fingertips until the mixture looks like crumbs. Mix in the skyr, quark or fromage frais. Knead the dough lightly with your hands just until the ingredients are amalgamated. Or put everything in a food processor and pulse-blend it together. In both cases, if the dough does not come together, sprinkle in a little water.

Roll the pastry out on a floured surface and butter a 28cm (11in) tart dish. Use the pastry to line the dish, then rest in the refrigerator for 1 hour.

Preheat the oven to 180°C/350°F/Gas Mark 4.

Cover the pastry case with baking parchment and fill with dried beans or raw rice. Bake in the hot oven for 15 minutes. Remove the paper and beans and bake for 5 minutes more.

Meanwhile, in a sauté pan, sauté the leeks and thyme in the butter until softened.

Lightly beat the eggs in a large mixing bowl, then add the crème fraîche, cheese, nutmeg and some salt and pepper and mix well. Fold in the leeks and season once more with salt and pepper.

Pour the mixture into the pastry case and return to the oven for 30–35 minutes, or until the filling is golden-brown, but retains a slight wobble. Allow to cool to room temperature before slicing.

BAKING ON A WHIM

There are many reasons why I will never tire of baking. The process is so tactile and the dough always so alive beneath my hands, meaning that baking is therapeutic in many ways… but it also connects me with history, and with my family's traditions, both of which give it a meaning that is quite separate from merely feeding people. Baking is so primal that, when you bake, it's as if you tap into a centuries-old meta-language.

Baking also connects us directly to nature: once a year – or twice in some places – grain is sowed and fields tended, plants grow, the harvest comes, the grains are dried and milled and some are saved as seeds for the next crop. And so it goes on, year after year of the grain-and-flour life cycle. Flour is never 'just flour', it's part of the circle that feeds us and is the result of the hard work of many souls over thousands of years.

Bread is made from flour, of course, so our daily bread ought to be the connecting dot that makes us stop and think about why protecting the land is essential, and to acknowledge that nature is always around us even when we live far away from grain fields. Nature takes care of the land and we need to help nature do its job, instead of interfering as we do now, because without a fertile healthy soil there will be no bread.

Civilization began when we stopped hunting and stayed put to grow grains, harvest, mill, cook and bake to survive. Bread has triggered revolutions, been used as peace offerings, and, in many countries around the world, it makes up the majority of the diet. Bread is baked in huge factories, niche artisan bakeries and at home; it can be steamed, baked in a small oven, or over an open fire. That simple combination of flour, salt and water comes in many forms and combinations.

Some of the best bread, I believe, is home baked. Even though I own a bakery now that bakes the greatest organic sourdough possible, I still crave my homemade spelt shower rolls, proved overnight for breakfast, my own seeded crispbreads with honey for cheese, my creamy vegetable filo pie when I crave comfort, and then – of course – on any rainy or cold day, a sweet rhubarb sticky bun. Baked things are so satisfying to eat, so homely.

When you are baking, time stops. You find yourself happily captured inside a bubble of natural wonders: the magic of dough rising, pastry caramelizing. It brings me joy to make a dough or pastry, place it in the oven and wait for the fragrance of baking to start spreading through the kitchen and then through the whole house, warm in the knowledge that soon something tasty will emerge for us all to eat and enjoy.

SEEDED CRISPBREADS WITH HONEY

These are great for lunch with a salad, or with cheese in the mornings, or added to a cheeseboard at night. Also, if you crave something sweet, eat them with chocolate-hazelnut spread, or try butter with raisins. They are a staple in my household, a very Scandinavian tradition dating back to when we had to bake bread that would last all through the winter.

MAKES 6

20g (¾oz) fresh yeast, or 7g (1½ tsp) fast-action (instant) dried yeast
200ml (generous ¾ cup) lukewarm water
1 tsp sea salt flakes (kosher salt)
1 tbsp honey
50ml (¼ cup) sunflower oil, plus more to brush (optional)
50g (1¾oz) linseeds (flaxseeds)
50g (1¾oz) sesame seeds
250g (9oz) plain (all-purpose) flour
150g (5½oz) stoneground wholemeal (wholewheat) rye flour

Dissolve the yeast in the lukewarm water in a mixing bowl, then add the salt, honey and oil and stir well.

In a separate bowl, mix the linseeds, sesame seeds and both flours.

Stir the wet mixture into the flour mixture until it forms a dough, then get your hand in and knead. It will be a firm dough, but still a bit sticky. Cover with a tea (dish) towel and let it rest for 30 minutes.

Preheat the oven to 220°C/425°F/Gas Mark 7.

Divide the dough into 6 pieces. Place a piece between 2 sheets of baking parchment and roll out into a round flatbread, as thin as possible. Relax: it doesn't have to be even, holes here and there are okay.

Place on a baking tray on the baking parchment it was rolled on, removing the top sheet. Repeat to roll out all the crackers. Depending on the size of your oven, you can bake 2–3 of these at a time.

Bake for 8–12 minutes, then brush with a little sunflower oil and cool on a wire rack. When cold, store in an airtight container. They will keep for up to 3 weeks.

SAFFRON LOAF

Saffron is regal. In Scandinavia, it used to be thought of as a romantic ingredient grown in faraway places… but that has changed. In Sweden, you can now find organic *österlensaffran* grown in Skåne. It is fragrant, beautiful and now – for me – local.

MAKES 1 LOAF

½ tsp saffron strands
50g (1¾oz) fresh yeast, or 15g (½oz) fast-action (instant) dried yeast
200ml (generous ¾ cup) whole milk, lukewarm
100g (3½oz) full-fat crème fraîche
2 tbsp honey
650g (1lb 7oz) strong white flour (white bread flour), plus more to dust
10g (2 tsp) sea salt flakes (kosher salt)
200g (2 sticks) salted butter, softened
1 egg, lightly beaten

Crush the saffron lightly in a mortar and pestle, add 2 tbsp hot water, stir, then leave for 10 minutes.

In a large bowl, dissolve the yeast in the lukewarm milk, then add the crème fraîche, honey and saffron water. Combine the flour and salt, then mix this into the yeast mixture.

Now knead in the butter, a little at a time, until you have a smooth dough. Return the dough to the bowl, cover with a tea (dish) towel and leave to rise for 90 minutes.

Tip the dough out on to a floured work surface and divide into 3 even balls. Roll each ball into a long sausage shape, then plait (braid) them into 1 loaf, pressing the pieces together at each end. Place in a 30 x 10cm (12 x 4in) loaf tin (bread pan), cover with a tea towel once more and leave to rise for 30 minutes.

Preheat the oven to 200°C/400°F/Gas Mark 6.

Brush the bread with the egg and bake for 45 minutes. If you think it is starting to get too dark in the oven, cover the loaf with foil or baking parchment. Tip the loaf out of its tin and knock lightly on the base: if it sounds hollow, it is done. Leave to cool on a wire rack for at least 30 minutes before cutting into it.

HOT FRIED SALT BREAD

A simple treat, these have to be fried as close as possible to the time they will be eaten. I like to serve them for parties: first I make drinks for my guests, then I cook these and pass them around as I fry them.

MAKES 36

25g (1oz) fresh yeast, or 7g (1½ tsp) fast-action (instant) dried yeast
200ml (generous ¾ cup) lukewarm water
450g (1lb) strong white flour (white bread flour) flour, plus more to dust
1 litre (1 quart) grapeseed oil, or other neutral-tasting oil, to deep-fry
sea salt flakes (kosher salt)

In a mixing bowl, dissolve the yeast in the lukewarm water. Add the flour and a pinch of salt and stir to bring together a dough.

Place the dough on a lightly floured work surface and knead until the dough is smooth and elastic. Place in a bowl, cover with a tea (dish) towel and leave to rise at room temperature for 1 hour.

Tip the dough on to a floured work surface, knead lightly, then divide into 4 portions. Roll each portion into a square, about 1cm (½in) thick. Cut each into 2cm (¾in) squares.

Heat the oil in a large pan until sizzling. Lower the pieces of dough into the hot oil in small batches, so the oil temperature remains steady. Cook for 2–3 minutes until golden.

Place the cooked hot fried bread on kitchen paper (paper towels) and generously sprinkle with sea salt flakes. Hand them around to your guests straight away, while you continue until all the dough has been fried.

BAGUETTE

Flour is never 'just flour'; it has multiple identities around the globe. I am very particular about it, and use organic flour from a local mill in Denmark. When I am baking, flavour is naturally very important to me, and you have to choose flour as carefully as you would wine, coffee or chocolate. Like all of these, flour has terroir, so look for your local organic miller and try their flour; I bet you notice a difference.

MAKES 4

For the starter

10g (¼oz) fresh yeast
250ml (1 cup plus 2 tsp) lukewarm water
200g (7oz) strong white flour (white bread flour)

For the dough

500ml (2 cups plus 4 tsp) cold water
750g (1lb 10½oz) strong white flour (white bread flour), plus more to dust
10g (2 tsp) sea salt flakes (kosher salt)

Day 1
Make the starter. Dissolve the yeast in the lukewarm water in a large bowl, add the flour and mix well. Cover the bowl with a tea (dish) towel and leave at room temperature for 3–4 hours.

After the 3–4 hours, make the dough. If you have a stand mixer use that fitted with the dough hook, otherwise do it by hand. Add the cold water to the yeast mixture, then the flour. Knead well with a dusting of flour, or run the stand mixer at low speed for 5 minutes. Now add the salt and knead well again, or run the stand mixer for 5 minutes. Cover the bowl with cling film (plastic wrap) and refrigerate overnight.

Day 2
The next day, preheat the oven to 220°C/425°F/Gas Mark 7. If you have a baking stone, put it in the oven to warm up.

Knead the dough lightly on a floured surface, divide into 4 and form each piece into a long baguette. Place on a very large baking sheet lined with baking parchment and slash the tops diagonally at intervals, using a razor or very sharp knife. Brush with water. If using a baking stone, slide the baguettes on to the hot stone. Otherwise just place the baking sheet in the oven. Bake for 20 minutes, then tap the bases – they should sound hollow. If not, bake for another 5 minutes. Leave to cool on a wire rack.

BUTTER STARS

These are sweet, salty and savoury all at the same time. They are a perfect snack on their own, or with creamy goat's cheese, or even as crackers to go alongside soup. It's important for me to warn you that you will eat them all in one sitting if you are not careful, they are kind of addictive.

MAKES 40–50

75ml (2¾fl oz) lukewarm water
10g (¼oz) fresh yeast, or 2g (½ tsp) fast-action (instant) dried yeast
1 egg, plus extra glaze, lightly beaten
100g (3½oz) stoneground spelt flour
300g (10½oz) stoneground wholemeal (wholewheat) flour
10g (¼oz) tsp salt
250g (2¼ sticks) cold salted butter, cubed
100g (3½oz) Cheddar cheese, very finely grated (shredded)

Mix the water, yeast and beaten egg in a bowl and set aside.

In another bowl, mix both types of flour with the salt. Rub the butter into the flour with your fingertips until the mixture resembles crumbs. Now add most of the cheese.

Add the yeast mixture, then knead the dough with your hands until it is soft but not too sticky. Shape the dough into a ball and chill for 1 hour.

Preheat the oven to 210°C/410°F/Gas Mark 6½.

Place the dough on a lightly floured work surface and divide it in half. Roll one half to about 3mm (⅛in) thick. Cut out into star-shaped biscuits (cookies) – or any other shape you want – with a cookie cutter. Place on a baking sheet lined with baking parchment. Repeat with the other half of the dough.

Lightly beat the remaining egg and brush it over each biscuit to glaze. Sprinkle with the reserved cheese.

Bake for 12–15 minutes, or until golden, then leave to cool on a wire rack. They will keep for 8 days in an airtight container.

Baking on a Whim

SPELT SHOWER ROLLS

These are a go-to recipe of mine, though I have changed the flours in recent years. Make the dough the night before and pop it into the refrigerator, then, when you wake up the next morning, take it out and bake the rolls while you take a shower. When you are finished, the rolls will be ready. The spelt makes them dense and full of fibre, with a sweet and savoury flavour.

MAKES 14–16

10g (¼oz) fresh yeast, or 5g (generous ½ tsp) fast-action (instant) dried yeast
600ml (2½ cups) cold water
1 tsp sea salt flakes (kosher salt)
450g (1lb) strong white flour (white bread flour), plus more to dust
300g (10½oz) wholemeal (wholewheat) spelt flour

Stir the yeast into the cold water in a bowl, add the salt, then mix in both the flours and give it a good stir with a wooden spoon. This is a very soft and sticky dough. Cover and place in the refrigerator overnight, or for at least 6 hours.

The next morning, preheat the oven to 220°C/425°F/Gas Mark 7. Line a baking sheet with baking parchment.

Take the dough out of the refrigerator and tip it out on to a floured work surface. Divide it into 14–16 pieces and form each into a roll; it will be sticky, but that's fine. Place them on the prepared baking sheet, spaced well apart.

Put the baking sheet in the oven, then immediately reduce the oven temperature to 210°C/410°F/Gas Mark 6½ and bake for 25–30 minutes.

Transfer the rolls to a wire rack for 5 minutes before serving them warm for breakfast!

RYE AND ONION PIZZAS WITH GOAT'S CHEESE

For cooking to be part of your everyday life, you need to plan. In fact, I think planning your weekly meals is the secret to a healthy life. Pizza is an excellent example of this: when we crave it, we often end up with a less-than-ideal frozen offering. Instead, decide which day you are going to have pizza for dinner, then take 10 minutes to mix the dough the evening before.

MAKES 2 / SERVES 2–4

For the dough
15g (½oz) fresh yeast, or 5g (1 tsp) fast-action (instant) dried yeast
50ml (¼ cup) sourdough starter (only if you have one up and running, otherwise leave it out)
300ml (1¼ cups) lukewarm water
450g (1lb) strong white flour (white bread flour), plus more to dust
150g (5½oz) stoneground wholemeal (wholewheat) rye flour
10g (2 tsp) sea salt flakes (kosher salt)

For the topping
2 tbsp olive oil
1 tbsp salted butter
500g (1lb 2oz) onions, each one sliced into 6 wedges
leaves from 5 thyme sprigs
100g (3½oz) goat's cheese
handful of parsley leaves, or rocket (arugula)
freshly ground black pepper

The evening before you want to eat your pizza, dissolve the yeast and sourdough starter (if using) in the lukewarm water in a large bowl. Mix in both flours and the salt and stir until the dough comes together. Knead lightly on a floured work surface until it is smooth, then put it in a large bowl, cover and leave to rise slowly in the refrigerator overnight.

The next day, preheat the oven to 200°C/ 400°F/Gas Mark 6.

Heat the oil and butter in a large frying pan (skillet) and sauté the onions with the thyme for 5 minutes, seasoning generously. Leave in the pan to cool down.

Divide the dough in half and roll each piece out on a floured work surface into a round pizza base. Place each base on a baking sheet lined with baking parchment. Now divide the sautéed onions between the pizzas and sprinkle with salt and pepper.

Bake for 20–25 minutes.

Remove the pizzas from the oven, crumble the goat's cheese over the top, then sprinkle each with the parsley or rocket. Serve right away.

BEAUTIFUL CAULIFLOWER
TREES ON FILO

Take a moment to stop and look, really look, at a cauliflower. It is beautiful and fascinating,
as well as shot through with texture. And, when cut into slices, a cauliflower looks like the tree
of life. So, instead of breaking cauliflower into little florets, in this recipe I slice it thinly to make
the beauty of the vegetable apparent.

MAKES 2 / SERVES 4

10 sheets of filo pastry (phyllo)
200g (2 scant sticks) salted butter, melted,
   for brushing
1 cauliflower
50g (1¾oz) hazelnuts, roughly chopped
4 tbsp chopped flat-leaf parsley leaves
sea salt flakes (kosher salt) and freshly ground
   black pepper

Preheat the oven to 200°C/400°F/Gas Mark 6.

Unfold the sheets of filo pastry, but keep
them covered with a damp tea (dish) towel as
you work, to prevent them from drying out.
Place a sheet of pastry on a work surface,
then gently brush it with melted butter. Place
another sheet on top of the first and brush
that with butter too. Repeat the process, so
you have 5 sheets of pastry forming a thicker
rectangle, brush the top sheet with butter too.
Repeat with a separate stack, so you have 2 filo
bases, each with 5 layers. Place each stack on a
baking sheet lined with baking parchment.

Rinse the cauliflower and take off all the
leaves, then cut it into thin slices from stalk to
tip, so the slices look like little treetops. Place
on the filo stacks, creating a beautiful pattern
and covering the pastry. Brush the cauliflower
with melted butter, then scatter over the
hazelnuts and sprinkle with salt and pepper.

Bake for 15 minutes. When the stacks come
out of the oven, scatter with parsley and serve
right away.

CREAMY VEGETABLE FILO PIE

Layers of crunch with a soft and flavourful filling, this is true comfort food
for any day you need it.

SERVES 4–6

100g (1 stick) salted butter, melted, plus 2 tbsp,
   plus more for the tin
5 sheets of filo pastry (phyllo)
1 garlic clove, finely chopped
1 leek, sliced and well washed (see page 30)
2 courgettes (zucchini), sliced
500g (1lb 2oz) spinach, rinsed well
200g (7oz) full-fat crème fraîche
150g (5½oz) Cheddar cheese, grated (shredded)
½ tsp freshly grated nutmeg
3 eggs, lightly beaten
sea salt flakes (kosher salt) and freshly ground
   black pepper

Preheat the oven to 200°C/400°F/Gas Mark 6.

Butter a 24cm (9½in) diameter springform tin
(pan), or other round baking tin.

Unfold the pastry, but keep it covered with a
damp tea (dish) towel as you work, to prevent
it from drying out. Place a filo sheet on a work
surface, then gently brush it with melted
butter. Place the next sheet at a slight angle
on the first, then brush it with butter. Repeat
the process, so the 5 sheets of pastry form a
more or less regular-shaped star. Place in the
prepared tin.

Melt the 2 tbsp butter in a sauté pan and sauté
the garlic, leek and courgettes for 5 minutes,
then add the spinach and let it cook for a few
minutes until wilted. Turn off the heat and
add the crème fraîche and cheese, seasoning
with the nutmeg and some salt and pepper.
Now add the eggs and stir well.

Spread the vegetable mixture in the filo pastry
case, folding the ends of the filo over the filling
to cover. Gently butter the top of the pie with
the last of the melted butter, then bake for
30 minutes. Allow to rest out of the oven for
a few moments before serving.

SWEET SUMMER BREAD

This bread is inspired by a cake that my grandma used to make. One summer, on a cloudy day, my mother and I were sitting on the terrace talking about how much I used to love that cake… then I decided to try to make a bread following the same idea. This is now the bread that I bake on rainy summer days.

SERVES 6–8

25g (1oz) fresh yeast, or 7g (1½ tsp) fast-action (instant) dried yeast
350ml (1½ cups) lukewarm water
1 egg, lightly beaten
350g (12oz) strong white flour (white bread flour), plus more to dust
150g (5½oz) wholemeal (wholewheat) spelt flour
1 tsp sea salt flakes (kosher salt)
100g (3½oz) raisins
100g (3½oz) dried figs, chopped
100g (3½oz) dried apricots, chopped
100g (3½oz) walnuts, chopped

To glaze
1 egg, lightly beaten
3 tbsp light brown sugar

Dissolve the yeast in the lukewarm water, add the egg, then stir in both the flours and the salt to form a wet dough. Add the raisins, figs, apricots and walnuts. Knead by hand for a few minutes, or in a stand mixer fitted with a dough hook, until smooth. Cover with a tea (dish) towel and leave to rise for 2 hours.

Preheat the oven to 200°C/400°F/Gas Mark 6.

Tip the dough out on to a floured work surface and knead lightly, then shape it into a round loaf. Line a 40 x 30cm (16 x 12in) baking sheet with baking parchment, then put the loaf on the sheet. Glaze with the beaten egg and sprinkle with the brown sugar.

Bake for 25–30 minutes, then remove from the baking tray and leave to cool on a wire rack.

RHUBARB STICKY BUNS

In Scandinavia, we are famous for our cinnamon and cardamom buns, made with a soft, yeasty dough. I decided to try them with rhubarb in place of the spices, since it is a local vegetable for me. Just like the original, these buns are soft, sweet and sticky.

MAKES 14–16

For the buns
300g (10½oz) rhubarb
100g (3½oz) caster (superfine) sugar
50g (1¾oz) fresh yeast, or 10g (2 tsp) fast-action
  (instant) dried yeast
200ml (generous ¾ cup) lukewarm whole milk
100g (3½oz) full-fat crème fraîche
1 egg, lightly beaten
650g (1lb 7oz) strong white flour (white bread
  flour), plus more to dust
1 tsp sea salt flakes (kosher salt)
100g (1 stick) salted butter, softened

For the filling
100g (3½oz) salted butter, softened
50g (1¾oz) caster (superfine) sugar
100g (3½oz) marzipan, grated (shredded)

Cut the rhubarb into 1cm (½in) pieces, place in a saucepan with 50g (1¾oz) of the sugar and bring to the boil. Cook for 5 minutes, then drain through a sieve placed over a heatproof bowl. Return the juice to the pan, bring to the boil once more and cook down until you have a syrup. Leave to cool.

Dissolve the yeast in the lukewarm milk in a bowl, then stir in the crème fraîche and egg. Next, mix in the flour, the remaining 50g (1¾oz) sugar and the salt. Knead the butter, little by little, into the dough, then knead well on a floured work surface until smooth.

Put the dough in a bowl, cover with a tea (dish) towel and let it rise for 1–2 hours, or until doubled in size.

Make the filling by mixing the butter, sugar and marzipan into a smooth paste.

Line some baking sheets with baking parchment.

Continued overleaf…

RHUBARB STICKY BUNS CONTINUED . . .

Tip the dough out on to a floured work surface and roll it into a rectangle measuring about 40 x 30cm (16 x 12in). Spread the filling evenly over half the dough, then arrange the cooked rhubarb pieces on top of the filling. Fold the plain side over the filled side, then cut across into 2cm (¾in) strips.

Take each strip and twist it, then roll each twist into a spiral.

Place the rhubarb buns on the prepared trays, pressing down on each so they spread slightly. Cover and leave to rise for 30 minutes.

Preheat the oven to 180°C/350°F/Gas Mark 4.

Bake the pastries for 25–30 minutes, then remove from the oven and brush with the rhubarb syrup. Leave to cool on a wire rack before serving.

BRUNSVIGER

This is a baking classic from Fyn, the island in the middle of Denmark where my family comes from, though it's a very regional item; it's almost impossible to buy them, for instance, in Copenhagen. When I was a girl, staying with my *mormor* (grandmother) on the island, we were allowed to choose a pastry for breakfast at the weekend and this would always be my choice. From the age of about 10 I started to bake them for myself, and, for my birthday one year, I baked it in a human shape and decorated it with candy! It is still my favourite choice for weekend breakfast. I can eat a lot of these...

SERVES 8

For the dough
50g (1¾oz) fresh yeast, or 10g (¼oz) fast-action (instant) dried yeast
200ml (generous ¾ cup) lukewarm whole milk
1 egg, lightly beaten, plus more to glaze
450g (1lb) plain (all-purpose) flour, plus more to dust
50g (1¾oz) caster (superfine) sugar
1 tsp ground cardamom seeds
½ tsp sea salt flakes (kosher salt)
150g (5½oz) salted butter, softened

For the topping
150g (5½oz) soft brown sugar
200g (7oz) salted butter, softened
50g (¼ cup) double (heavy) cream

Crumble the yeast into the milk and stir to dissolve, then add the egg. Mix the flour, sugar, cardamom and salt in a mixing bowl, then rub the butter into the flour with your fingers until it looks like crumbs. Stir the milk mixture into the flour mixture, then knead well on a floured surface. Put the dough into a bowl, cover with a tea (dish) towel and let it rise for 1–2 hours, or until doubled in size.

Line a 40 x 30cm (16 x 12in) baking tin with baking parchment. Tip the dough into the tin, encouraging it into the corners, then cover with a tea towel and leave to rise again for 30 minutes.

Preheat the oven to 200°C/400°F/Gas Mark 6.

Make the topping in a small saucepan by melting together the brown sugar, butter and cream. Mix well, then leave to cool a little.

When the dough has risen, press deep holes into it with your fingers. Spread the topping over it evenly, making sure some of it runs into the holes you made.

Bake for 25–30 minutes, then leave to cool on a wire rack for 30 minutes before slicing into squares and eating.

BEACH
PARTY

Eating outside is always better: a picnic, dinner in the front yard, or a tea break on a walk in autumn, sitting on a bench with tea in a thermos flask and sharing a sandwich. That is bliss for me, sign me up for any outdoor eating! Cooking outside is also something I enjoy immensely and I started cooking over open fires more seriously five years ago. I have still not mastered it 100 per cent, but I keep practising and I learn something new each time. Living in Copenhagen means that cooking over open flame is only something I can do when I'm at the beach or in the countryside.

A beach party on a long Scandinavian summer night is truly unforgettable. The fine sandy beach, the cool clear water, the beautiful light and the fact that there are so many beaches and so few people on them, you have the stunning space all to yourself.

To prepare for a beach party, I start in the kitchen, prepping everything. At the beach, I set up my food and equipment, build the fire, take my last swim, then light the fire and pass the drinks around. People come early, so everyone shares the whole process, swims and hangs out, but also sees the light changing as the day turns to dusk and then silently melts away. That half-light is the moment of the day when I feel most connected to the elements.

When the fire is ready, you let the elements take over and adapt to them. I bake bread, add vegetables to the glowing embers, then I walk into the sea to get some newspaper wet and wrap it around the fish, tucking in some herbs and lemon. I let vegetables sizzle in a pan over the fire, everybody gathers around and we watch the sunset, while I feed people as the food is ready.

As the air gets cooler, we move closer to the fire. I boil water and make coffee, serve pudding and we all enjoy the sky turning from blue to orange and then to dark pink. This is Scandinavia remember, so there is always a ray of light on the horizon, it's never pitch black in the summer.

I bring blankets and warm sweaters from the beach house, so we end the evening cosily around the fire, sipping local calvados and gazing into the sky, letting the stars tell the rest of the story.

STRAWBERRY
CAMPARI SPRITZ

SERVES 6

300g (10½oz) fresh strawberries
250ml (1 cup) Campari
500g (2 cups) sparkling water
6 lime slices
plenty of ice cubes

For the strawberry syrup
500g (1lb 2oz) frozen strawberries
150g (5½oz) caster (superfine) sugar
100ml (scant ½ cup) water

First make the syrup. Place the ingredients in a saucepan, bring to the boil, then reduce the heat and let it simmer for 30 minutes. Pour into a sieve placed over a bowl and press as much juice out as possible. Discard the strawberry pulp left in the sieve, then leave the syrup to cool.

Place the fresh strawberries in a jar and, with a muddler or wooden spoon, mash them up a little, then add the Campari and 50ml (¼ cup) of the strawberry syrup. Stir and add the sparkling water, lime slices and ice cubes. Stir again, then serve right away.

Store any leftover strawberry syrup in the refrigerator. It can be added to other drinks, or just to sparkling water, or used as a sauce for ice cream.

MUSSELS WITH
CELERIAC AND CABBAGE

My Scandinavian mussel dish contains about as many vegetables as it does mussels! It's perfect for cooking either over a fire or in your kitchen, and works both for an everyday dinner or for a weekend dinner party.

SERVES 6

1kg (2lb 4oz) mussels
2 tbsp salted butter
3 garlic cloves, finely chopped
2 leeks, sliced and well washed (see page 30)
1 celeriac (celery root), finely chopped
2 carrots, finely chopped
½ Savoy cabbage, finely chopped
200g (generous ¾ cup) crème fraîche
2–4 tbsp lemon juice
large bunch of flat-leaf parsley, finely chopped
sea salt flakes (kosher salt) and freshly ground
   black pepper

Scrub the mussels thoroughly and tug out any beards that may be hanging from the shells. Discard any broken or open mussels, or any that are open and refuse to close when the shell is tapped, then rinse them in cold water a couple of times.

In a large pot, melt the butter and sauté the garlic and leeks for a few minutes, then add the celeriac and carrots and sprinkle with salt and pepper. Cover and let it cook for 5 minutes. Now add the mussels and mix in with the vegetables. Cover with a lid and let it cook for a further 5 minutes.

Remove the lid and add the cabbage and crème fraîche. Mix well and let simmer for a few minutes, then season to taste with lemon juice and more salt and pepper. Sprinkle with the parsley and serve right away.

FLATBREAD ON THE FIRE

This is a very easy dough to prepare, and making bread over a fire is such a delight. *Everything* you eat outside seems to taste better.

MAKES 10

50g (1¾oz) fresh yeast, or 10g (¼oz) fast-action (instant) dried yeast
500g (1lb 2oz) strong white flour (white bread flour), plus more to dust
2 tsp fine sea salt
350ml (1½ cups) water
extra virgin olive oil, to serve

In a large mixing bowl, rub the fresh yeast, if using, into the flour with your fingertips, or just mix through the dried yeast. Add the salt and water, then mix with your hands until a dough starts to form.

Place the dough on a lightly floured work surface and form it into a ball by folding each edge in turn into the centre. Place in a mixing bowl and cover with a tea (dish) towel. Rest for 1 hour in a warm, draught-free place.

Turn the dough out gently on to a well-floured work surface. Now form 10 small balls and roll them out into flatbreads. Generously flour the top of each, cover with a clean tea towel and set aside to rest once more for 5 minutes.

Lift each flatbread on to a lightly floured baking tray and take it to the barbecue. The barbecue should have burned down and the coals be glowing and pale.

Cook the flatbreads for 10–12 minutes until golden brown on both sides, then take off the fire, brush immediately with olive oil and eat.

BEACH SALAD

This is a light and easy salad to make and to eat at any picnic. It is very refreshing with fish (see page 174), and also acts as a great palate cleanser after the rich mussels (page 167).

SERVES 6

500g (1lb 2oz) white cabbage
150g (5½oz) kale
1 head of radicchio

For the dressing
2 tbsp white wine vinegar
1 tbsp lemon juice
1 tsp Dijon mustard
1 tsp honey
½ small garlic clove, finely grated (shredded)
4 tbsp extra virgin olive oil
sea salt flakes (kosher salt) and freshly ground
  black pepper

Rinse all the vegetables, then slice into thin strips and toss them in a big salad bowl.

Now make the dressing. Whisk together the vinegar, lemon juice, mustard, honey and garlic to a smooth paste in a mixing bowl, then gradually whisk in the oil. Season to taste with salt and pepper.

Just before eating, toss the salad with the dressing.

A FISH ON THE FIRE

This is a wonderfully simple way to cook and enjoy a whole fish. Tear open the paper once the fish is ready and allow everyone to dig in.

SERVES 6

1 large trout, or salmon, gutted and cleaned
3 flat-leaf parsley sprigs
about 10 sheets of old newspaper
6 lemons
sea salt flakes (kosher salt) and freshly ground
   black pepper

Take the fish and place the parsley inside the cavity, then sprinkle with salt and pepper inside and out.

Soak the newspaper in water (sea water is fine), then wrap the fish in the paper. Cut the lemons in half.

Place the newspaper-wrapped fish on a wire rack on top of the fire. Let it cook for 30–45 minutes, turning it 2–3 times. Place the lemons on the rack, cut sides down, and barbecue these as well until they are golden brown.

Keep the fish wrapped in the newspaper until you are ready to serve it. Serve with parsley-almond pesto and yogurt sauce (see page 177) and the charred lemons on the side for squeezing.

PARSLEY-ALMOND PESTO

SERVES 6

50g (1¾oz) curly parsley
50g (1¾oz) basil
50g (1¾oz) almonds
1 garlic clove
100ml (scant ½ cup) sunflower oil
2–3 tbsp lemon juice, plus more to taste
sea salt flakes (kosher salt) and freshly ground
    black pepper

Blend all the ingredients in a food processor to a smooth paste. Season to taste with salt, pepper and more lemon juice.

YOGURT SAUCE

SERVES 6

50g (1¾oz) curly parsley
400g (14oz) 10 per cent fat (full-fat) Greek yogurt
juice of ¼ lemon
1 tbsp Dijon mustard
sea salt flakes (kosher salt) and freshly ground
    black pepper

Blend the parsley in a food processor, so it becomes super-finely chopped (or do this by hand), then place in a mixing bowl and add the rest of the ingredients. Mix, then season to taste with salt and pepper.

BARBECUED
VEGETABLES AND TOAST

Charring vegetables like this is one of the best ways to enjoy them, especially with chunks of lovely bread on the side to scoop them up with.

SERVES 6

2 large heads of broccoli
2 fennel bulbs
1 loaf of sourdough bread
4 onions, halved
8 leeks
olive oil
sea salt flakes (kosher salt) and freshly ground
    black pepper

Cut the broccoli and fennel into big chunks and slice the sourdough bread.

Brush all the vegetable pieces and the whole leeks with olive oil, sprinkle with salt and pepper and grill them on a wire rack over the fire, turning to cook them on all sides until softened and charred.

Toast the bread in the same way, then top the toasts with the barbecued veggies and perhaps a dollop of yogurt sauce (see page 177).

GOOSEBERRY TRIFLE

After a warm summer's day at the beach comes a cool summer night. After our last swim, we gather around the fire. This is a highlight of the Scandinavian summer, when you can be outside late in the light. After the barbecue, blankets and warm clothes come out, we all get cosy around the fire and it's time for pudding! Trifle is a great choice, as it's light and sweet with some acidity, and – as it is August – gooseberry is my choice of fruit. The night doesn't end before midnight and we spend hours just staring up into the stars.

SERVES 6

For the compote
600g (1lb 5oz) gooseberries
1 vanilla pod (bean), split
200g (7oz) caster (superfine) sugar

For the crunch
100g (3½oz) caster (superfine) sugar
150g (5½oz) jumbo oats
50g (1¾oz) hazelnuts, roughly chopped
50g (½ stick) salted butter

To serve
200g (generous ¾ cup) double (heavy) cream

For the gooseberry compote, place the gooseberries in a saucepan with the split vanilla pod and let them simmer over a low heat for about 5 minutes. Add the sugar, stir well and let it simmer for another 10 minutes. Leave to cool, then store in jars in the refrigerator. It will keep for 2–3 weeks.

Preheat the oven to 180°C/350°F/Gas Mark 4.

Mix the sugar, oats and hazelnuts and place on a baking tray. Divide the butter into small pats and spread it over the mixture. Bake in the oven for 5 minutes, then mix the crunch well and bake for another 5–10 minutes, or until golden brown.

Whip the cream until it forms soft peaks.

Choose 6 glasses or jars. Spoon in alternate layers of gooseberry compote, cream and crunch, finishing with a swirl of cream on top.

THERE IS ALWAYS ROOM FOR SOMETHING SWEET

I love a sweet bun with a late-morning weekend breakfast. I adore afternoon cake with a cup of tea, but always with company; it's a convivial thing to do. Sometimes it's great to buy your sweet things in: a fruit tart, for instance, or, when travelling, a madeleine in Paris or a frosted carrot cake in New York City. Some cakes, though, are best made yourself; I think anything with cream is best homemade, as shop-bought ones are often too sweet and have too much cream.

I will walk many miles for nice artisanal ice cream; indeed I have trekked around many Italian cities in search of the perfect gelato, trying all the different flavours and being overwhelmed with joy when one of them just hits my sweet spot.

I like to indulge in a dessert after dinner, a sweet thing that completes a meal and makes it perfect. The punctuation mark that leads up to coffee. There is something ever-beguiling in the ritual of how even a midweek meal runs its course, that last part when you lay the napkin on the table, let the chair slide back, relax, let the conversation quieten down and enjoy your dessert.

I don't remember eating my first ever cake, though I think it must have been baked by my *mormor*. I do, though, remember when I baked my first cake without adults around; I sat on the floor in front of the oven and waited for it to be done. There was no glass front, so I had to get up now and then to open the oven door and peer inside. At some point, I decided it was done, but it was heavy, sticky, weird, over-sweet and doughy. Nevertheless, I ate it with gusto and served it proudly to the grown-ups in the commune we lived in. Despite that first cake, I kept baking, and over the years learned and understood the different baking techniques and experienced the incredibly satisfying sensation of getting the right balance in both flavour and texture.

A lot has changed over the course of my life, but not the cakes. They remain steadfast, an unshakable testimony to family, tradition and memories. Baking them is an easy way to time-travel, to recall birthdays, weddings and other celebrations, or indeed all the ordinary days when cake was needed.

I like my cakes to be simple, rustic and not too sweet, either fruity and acidic, or with some other kind of an edge. And, of course, homemade: the absolute best. I admire the elaborate work of professional bakeries, but my heart is with the simple, the humble and the homespun.

BLOOD ORANGE CHEESECAKE

We get blood oranges from Sicily in the wintertime. They are the most wonderful things, dark
red and orange in colour, sweet, sour and incredibly juicy. Each time I cut a fruit open,
I am in awe at what nature has to offer us.

SERVES 8

For the base
125g (4½oz) digestive biscuits (graham crackers)
150g (5½oz) salted butter, plus more for the tin
50g (1¾oz) light brown sugar
100g (3½oz) rye flakes
pinch of sea salt flakes (kosher salt)

For the filling
3 gelatine sheets
600g (1lb 5oz) full-fat cream cheese
75g (2¾oz) caster (superfine) sugar
150g (5½oz) double (heavy) cream
finely grated (shredded) zest of 1 blood orange

For the topping
3 gelatine sheets
300ml (1¼ cups) blood orange juice,
   from 8–10 blood oranges
1 tbsp caster (superfine) sugar

To serve
100ml (3½fl oz) blood orange juice
50g (1¾oz) caster (superfine) sugar
sliced segments from about 4 blood oranges

Preheat the oven to 160°C/325°F/Gas Mark 3.

Blitz the digestive biscuits in a food processor.
Cut the butter into cubes and add to the
biscuits with the brown sugar, rye flakes and
pinch of salt. Let the food processor run until
you have a smooth, sticky dough.

Line a 24cm (9½in) springform cake tin
(pan) with baking parchment, then butter the
parchment. Now, with a spatula, spread the
sticky dough out evenly to line the base of
the tin.

Bake for 20 minutes, then place on a wire rack
and leave until fully cold.

Soften the gelatine sheets for the filling in a
small bowl of cold water for about 5 minutes.
Beat the cream cheese and sugar until light
and fluffy using an electric whisk. Bring the
cream to the boil in a small saucepan, then
turn off the heat.

Remove the gelatine sheets from the water,
squeeze out the excess water, then place into
the hot cream, whisking to make sure the sheets
have fully dissolved and there are no lumps.
Now pour the cream mixture into the cream
cheese, beating constantly to make sure it is
well combined. Finally, fold in the orange zest.

Continued overleaf...

Pour the mixture over the cold cheesecake crust and spread it out evenly. Cover and place in the refrigerator for 3–4 hours.

Check the cheesecake has set: it needs to be firm when gently pushed with a finger. If so, it is ready for the topping.

Soften the gelatine sheets for the topping in a small bowl of cold water for about 5 minutes. Pour the blood orange juice into a small saucepan and add the sugar. Bring to the boil, then remove from the heat.

Remove the gelatine sheets from the water, squeeze out the excess water and place them in the hot orange juice, whisking to make sure the sheets have fully dissolved and there are no lumps. Very gently, pour the liquid on top of the cheesecake to cover. Cover the cheesecake again and return it to the refrigerator for another 3 hours, so the orange jelly sets.

Meanwhile, combine the blood orange juice with the caster sugar in a small saucepan and bring to the boil. Allow it to simmer for 5 minutes, then remove from the heat. Place the blood orange segments in a serving bowl and, once cool, pour the syrup over them.

Run a sharp knife around the edge of the cheesecake, carefully release the side of the tin and serve, with the blood oranges in syrup on the side.

CHILLED BUTTERMILK SOUP WITH STRAWBERRIES AND MERINGUES

This is the perfect dessert for a hot summer's day, when you are not that hungry and just want something cold and refreshing. It can be served with Croutons (see page 23) instead of meringues, if you prefer.

SERVES 4

For the meringues
4 egg whites
200g (7oz) caster (superfine) sugar

For the soup
1 vanilla pod (bean)
4 egg yolks
50g (1¾oz) caster (superfine) sugar
100ml (scant ½ cup) elderflower cordial
finely grated (shredded) zest and juice of
   1 lemon, plus more lemon juice to taste
1.5 litres (1.5 quarts) buttermilk
pinch of sea salt flakes (kosher salt)

To serve
500g (1lb 2oz) strawberries

Preheat the oven to 110°C/225°F/Gas Mark ¼.

Start by making the meringue. Whisk the egg whites until stiff, then gradually add the sugar, whisking all the time until all the sugar has dissolved. Take 2 baking sheets and line them with baking parchment, then dollop on large meringues. Bake in the oven for 90 minutes. Cool down on a wire rack, then place in an airtight container; they will keep for weeks.

Make the cold soup a few hours before serving. Split the vanilla pod lengthways and scrape out the seeds with the tip of a knife. In a bowl and using an electric whisk, beat the vanilla seeds with the egg yolks and sugar until pale yellow and fluffy. Add the elderflower cordial, lemon zest and juice, buttermilk and the pinch of salt, then season to taste with more lemon juice, if you like. Cover and chill for at least 1 hour.

Rinse the strawberries, hull them, then chop.

Serve the cold buttermilk soup with chopped strawberries and the meringues broken over the top.

There Is Always Room for Something Sweet

WINTER *ISLAGKAGE*

Islagkage is an ice-cream cake, very popular for birthdays as well as on New Year's Eve. You can order the cakes at specialist ice-cream shops or patisseries. This is easy to make at home, because it contains a parfait, not an ice cream, so you do not need to churn it or use an ice-cream machine. I think it tastes amazing and it will impress whoever you serve it to.

SERVES 6–8

For the sponge
salted butter, for the tin
4 eggs, separated
120g (4½oz) caster (superfine) sugar
30g (1oz) cocoa powder, sifted
pinch of sea salt flakes (kosher salt)

For the parfait
100g (3½oz) dried figs
100g (3½oz) candied orange peel (for homemade, see page 221)
100g (3½oz) raisins
50g (1¾oz) almonds
6 egg yolks
125g (4½oz) caster (superfine) sugar
600g (1lb 5oz) double (heavy) cream

For the caramel
100g (3½oz) white granulated sugar

Preheat the oven to 180°C/350°F/Gas Mark 4. Line a round 24cm (9½in) springform cake tin (pan) with baking parchment and butter the baking parchment.

Whisk the egg whites until stiff using an electric whisk, then whisk in half the sugar little by little until the egg whites are shiny and stiff. Whisk the egg yolks with the other half of the sugar until fluffy and pale yellow, then stir in the cocoa powder and the pinch of salt. Fold the beaten egg whites into the egg yolk mixture. Spread the mixture evenly in the tin and bake for 10 minutes. Allow to cool in the tin.

For the parfait, mix the figs, candied peel, raisins and almonds, then finely chop. Beat the egg yolks and sugar in a bowl with an electric whisk until pale yellow and fluffy. In a separate bowl, whip the cream until soft peaks form. Very gently fold the whipped cream into the beaten egg yolk mixture. Then fold the fruit and nut mixture into the cream.

Melt the sugar for the caramel in a heavy-based pan until golden brown, then drizzle it directly into the cream. Mix thoroughly, then pour the cream into the tin on top of the cooled sponge.

Wrap with cling film (plastic wrap) or foil, then freeze for 24 hours before serving. Take the ice-cream cake out 15 minutes before serving.

There Is Always Room for Something Sweet

SUMMER *ISLAGKAGE*

Here in Scandinavia, summer food is all about the berries. We are famous for them, juicy, sweet and not too big. My summer *islagkage* is with strawberries and elderflower. Let the parfait defrost a little before serving, so that the frozen chopped strawberries will not be as hard as stones!

SERVES 6

For the sponge
salted butter, for the tin
4 eggs, separated
120g (4½oz) caster (superfine) sugar
30g (1oz) cocoa powder
pinch of sea salt flakes (kosher salt)

For the parfait
1 vanilla pod (bean)
6 egg yolks
125g (4½oz) caster (superfine) sugar
100ml (scant ½ cup) elderflower cordial
600g (1lb 5oz) double (heavy) cream
300g (10½oz) strawberries, hulled and quartered

Preheat the oven to 180°C/350°F/Gas Mark 4. Make and bake the sponge (see page 195), then leave in the tin (pan) until cool.

To make the parfait, slice the vanilla pod in half lengthways, then scrape out the seeds with the tip of a knife. In a bowl, using an electric whisk, beat the egg yolks, sugar and vanilla seeds until fluffy and pale yellow, then whisk in the elderflower cordial. In a separate bowl, whip the cream until light and fluffy, then fold it into the egg mixture.

Fold the strawberries into the cream, then pour into the tin on top of the cooled sponge.

Wrap with cling film (plastic wrap) or foil, then freeze for 24 hours before serving. Take the ice-cream cake out 15 minutes before serving.

FASTELAVNSBUN

On the last Monday in February, we celebrate carnival in Denmark. The children get into costume, we hang wooden barrels up full of candy and confetti, and then, with clubs, the children take turns trying to break the barrels open, spilling their treasures to the ground. When that is done and the children have claimed their prizes, we eat *fastelavnsbun*.

MAKES 16

25g (1oz) fresh yeast, or 7g (1½ tsp) fast-action (instant) dried yeast
150ml (generous ½ cup) lukewarm water
1 egg, lightly beaten, plus 1 more for the glaze
1 tbsp caster (superfine) sugar
½ tsp sea salt flakes (kosher salt)
325g (11½oz) strong white flour (white bread flour), plus more to dust
300g (scant 3 sticks) salted butter, chilled, in thin slices

For the filling
100g (1 stick) salted butter, softened
100g (3½oz) caster (superfine) sugar
50g (1¾oz) almonds, finely chopped

For the cream
1 vanilla pod (bean)
600ml (2½ cups) whipping cream
4 tbsp icing (powdered) sugar
1 jar of jam, either gooseberry or blackcurrant

For the pink dust
50g (1¾oz) freeze-dried raspberries
150g (5½oz) icing (powdered) sugar

Dissolve the yeast in a bowl in the lukewarm water and add the beaten egg, the sugar and salt. Stir in the flour and knead the dough with your hands until it is even and light. Put it in a bowl, cover with a plate or lid and let it chill in the refrigerator for 15 minutes.

Roll out the dough on a floured work surface into a rough 45cm (18in) square. Form the slices of butter into a square half that size and place it in the centre of the dough at a 45° angle, so it forms a small diamond inside the pastry square. Fold the corners of the pastry over the butter to encase it fully and seal the joins well. Roll out the dough again carefully, this time into a rectangle, making sure that it does not crack and expose the butter.

Fold one of the short ends over into the centre by one-third, and the other short end over that: you are folding the rectangle into 3, as you would with a letter. Cover with a tea (dish) towel and let it rest in the refrigerator for 15 minutes.

Repeat this rolling and folding procedure 3 times in total, turning it by 90° each time before rolling it out again and remembering to let the dough chill for 15 minutes in the refrigerator between each turn. Now the dough is ready.

Continued overleaf…

There Is Always Room for Something Sweet

While the dough is resting, make the filling by mixing the butter, sugar and almonds in a bowl into a soft paste.

Roll the dough out into a 40cm (16in) square. Now cut it into sixteen 10cm (4in) squares. Place a dollop of the filling on each. Take the 4 corners of a dough square and fold them over the filling. Pinch the seams of dough together, then turn over so the seam sides are on the base. Repeat to form all the buns. Leave to prove on a baking tray lined with baking parchment for 30 minutes.

Preheat the oven to 200°C/400°F/Gas Mark 6.

Lightly beat the egg for the glaze, then brush each bun with the egg and bake for 18 minutes. Cool down on a wire rack.

When the pastries have cooled to room temperature, make the cream. Cut the vanilla pod in half lengthways and scrape out the seeds with the tip of a knife, then add the seeds to the cream and icing sugar in a bowl. Whip until it is billowing.

To make the pink dust, blitz the freeze-dried raspberries in a food processor or spice grinder to a powder, then sift this into the icing sugar and stir to combine. This will make far more than you need for this recipe but it will keep for up to 2 months in an airtight container.

Take each bun and cut it in half. Spread your chosen jam over the bottom half, then spread the cream on top. Place the top half of the bun on the cream, then dust with pink dust.

MEDALJER

A pink treat that will make you calm and happy! Pink is my favourite colour, which may be banal, but it's true and it has been all my life. One way to indulge this is in cake!

MAKES 10

For the pastry
200g (7oz) plain (all-purpose) flour, plus more
   to dust
50g (1¾oz) icing (powdered) sugar
1 tsp finely grated (shredded) lemon zest
100g (1 stick) salted butter, chilled and chopped
½ egg, lightly beaten

For the icing and decoration
100g (3½oz) icing (powdered) sugar
2–3 tbsp cordial, strawberry, raspberry, or any red
   berry flavour

For the filling
1 vanilla pod (bean)
200g (7oz) double (heavy) cream
100g (3½oz) icing (powdered) sugar
200g (7oz) raspberries

To make the pastry, sift the flour and icing sugar into a bowl and add the lemon zest. Rub the butter into the dry ingredients until the mixture resembles crumbs. Add the egg and stir until the pastry comes together. Wrap in cling film (plastic wrap) and chill for 30 minutes.

Preheat the oven to 220°C/425°F/Gas Mark 7. Line a baking tray with baking parchment.

Roll out the pastry on a floured work surface to a thickness of 2–3mm (⅛in). Use a 6–7cm (2½–2¾in) diameter pastry cutter, or the rim of a similar-sized glass, to cut the pastry into 20 discs. Spread them out on the prepared tray and bake for 6–7 minutes, then transfer carefully (they are a bit fragile) to a wire rack to cool.

To make the icing, sift the icing sugar into a small bowl, add the cordial and whisk until you have a smooth paste. Take half the biscuits and spread the icing on top, keeping it a few millimetres from the edge. Set aside until the icing has set.

For the filling, split the vanilla pod lengthways and scrape out the seeds with the tip of a knife. Put the seeds in a mixing bowl with the cream and icing sugar and whip until light and fluffy, then fold in the raspberries.

Place the un-iced biscuits on a work surface and spread with the raspberry cream, then top with the iced biscuits. Serve immediately.

There Is Always Room for Something Sweet

AUTUMN PEAR PIE
WITH HAZELNUT PASTRY

I like to use Bosc pears for this, as they are firm, but most firm pears can be used. The pie will taste good cold for days, but can also be reheated and served warm on the second or third day after it is baked.

SERVES 6–8

For the pastry
100g (3½oz) hazelnuts
275g (9¾oz) plain (all-purpose) flour,
   plus more to dust
225g (2 sticks) salted butter, chopped
50g (1¾oz) icing (powdered) sugar
1 egg, lightly beaten, plus 1 more to glaze

For the filling
6 pears
1 vanilla pod (bean)
1 tbsp caster (superfine) sugar
100ml (scant ½ cup) water

To serve
200g (7oz) full-fat crème fraîche

Blitz the hazelnuts in a food processor until they resemble flour, then mix with the plain flour. Rub the butter into the flour until it resembles crumbs, then stir in the sugar. Mix in the beaten egg to form a ball, then cut the dough in half. On a floured work surface, roll out half the pastry until it's big enough to line a 24cm (9½in) tart tin (pan), then use it to line the tin. Wrap the other half in cling film (plastic wrap), then chill both in the refrigerator for 1 hour.

Peel the pears and cut in them half, then remove the cores. Split the vanilla pod lengthways, scrape the seeds out with the tip of a knife and place in a saucepan with the pears, sugar and water. Bring to the boil, then reduce the heat to a simmer for 5 minutes. Turn the heat off and leave the pears to cool in the pan.

Preheat the oven to 180°C/350°F/Gas Mark 4.

Line the chilled pastry case with a piece of baking parchment and fill it with dried beans or raw rice. Bake for 10 minutes, then remove from the oven and remove the beans and parchment. Meanwhile, roll the remaining pastry out into a circle big enough to cover the pie.

Place the pears tightly in the pastry case, cut sides down, and cover with the circle of uncooked pastry, pressing the edges to seal. Lightly beat the remaining egg and use it to brush the top. Bake for 25 minutes. Rest the pie for 15 minutes before serving warm, with crème fraîche.

There Is Always Room for Something Sweet

MADELEINES WITH REDCURRANTS

Would madeleines be a thing if they had not been mentioned in Proust's famous novel? I think so. Of course they are best just out of the oven; I can eat several warm madeleines in a single sitting! I also like them when they are up to five days old, dipped in my tea in the afternoon. I believe they should be eaten in the afternoon, just before dusk.

MAKES 18

2 large eggs
80g (2¾oz) caster (superfine) sugar
20g (¾oz) light brown sugar
80g (2¾oz) strong white flour (white bread flour),
   plus more for the tin
½ tsp baking powder
20g (¾oz) honey
100g (1 stick) salted butter, melted, plus more
   for the tin
finely grated (shredded) zest of 1 lemon
100g (3½oz) redcurrants

Beat the eggs with both the sugars using an electric whisk until fluffy and pale yellow. Sift in the flour and baking powder and fold lightly into the egg mix, then, with a hand whisk, whisk in the honey, melted butter and lemon zest. Leave to chill in the refrigerator for at least 2 hours.

When the batter is ready, preheat the oven to 210°C/410°F/Gas Mark 6½. Butter and flour 18 holes of a regular-sized madeleine tin (pan).

Fold the redcurrants into the batter and pour it into the prepared tin, only to just beneath the rim of the moulds, or it will run over when baking.

Bake for 8–10 minutes, until golden brown, then allow to cool a little before you eat the first madeleine. Any that you don't eat straight away (more challenging than you might think) can be stored in an airtight container for up to 1 week.

HONEY-SPICE MUFFINS

If you like any spiced cake, such as gingerbread, then these muffins are to die for. I love spiced cakes and always used to make a kind of gingerbread loaf with buttercream. Then some years back, when I opened Hahnemanns bakery, we developed this recipe from my gingerbread loaf recipe. I love it and it is fun to make with the children in my family. So, these muffins are now one of the highlights of my Copenhagen winter.

MAKES 16

For the muffins
butter, for the tins (optional)
4 eggs, separated
100g (3½oz) soft brown sugar
225g (8oz) honey
250g (9oz) strong white flour (white bread flour)
2 tsp baking powder
½ tsp ground cinnamon
½ tsp ground cloves
½ tsp ground ginger

For the buttercream
350g (generous 3 sticks) salted butter
350g (12oz) icing (powdered) sugar

To decorate
200g (7oz) dark chocolate, 60–70 per cent cocoa
    solids, broken up
jar of apricot jam
Mini Gingerbread Men (see overleaf), or edible
    lustre (both optional)

Start by baking the muffins. Butter 16 muffin moulds, unless you are using silicone moulds, which do not need to be buttered. As muffin tins (pans) usually come in 12s, you will need 2 tins for this recipe. Preheat the oven to 170°C/340°F/Gas Mark 3½.

Using an electric whisk or a stand mixer, beat the egg yolks, sugar and honey until light and fluffy. Sift together the flour, baking powder and spices, then fold them into the egg mixture. Separately beat the egg whites until stiff, using an electric whisk or a stand mixer with clean beaters, then fold gently into the batter.

Now pour the mixture into the prepared moulds and bake for 25–30 minutes. Test with a skewer to see if the muffins are done: it should emerge clean with no batter. Let the muffins cool on a wire rack.

For the buttercream, use an electric whisk or a food mixer to beat the butter until light and creamy. Gradually add the icing sugar and beat on a low speed for 3 minutes. Scrape down the sides of the bowl and beat for another 5 minutes, then spoon it into a piping bag fitted with either a star or a plain nozzle (tip).

Continued overleaf...

HONEY-SPICE MUFFINS CONTINUED . . .

Melt the chocolate in a heatproof bowl placed over a saucepan of simmering water, making sure the bowl does not touch the water.

Now you are ready to put the muffins together. Carefully slice the top off each muffin and dip it in the melted chocolate. Place, chocolate sides up, on a sheet of baking parchment and allow the chocolate to set.

Place the bottom parts of the muffins on a tray. Pipe a ring of buttercream around the edge of each muffin base. Spoon a heaped teaspoon of apricot jam inside the rings of buttercream. Place the set chocolate muffin tops on top of the cream.

Now pipe a small dollop of buttercream on top, and add a mini gingerbread man or a dusting of edible lustre.

The muffins will keep for 3–4 days at room temperature in an airtight container.

FOR THE MINI GINGERBREAD MEN

MAKES 16

50ml (¼ cup) golden syrup
100g (3½oz) soft brown sugar
½ tsp ground ginger
½ tsp ground cinnamon
60g (½ stick) salted butter, softened
50ml (¼ cup) single (light) cream
250g (9oz) plain (all-purpose) flour,
   plus more to dust
¼ tsp bicarbonate of soda (baking soda)

Preheat the oven to 200°C/400°F/Gas Mark 6.
Line a baking sheet with baking parchment.

In a mixing bowl and using an electric whisk,
beat together the syrup, sugar, spices and
softened butter. Add the cream and mix again.
Sift in the flour and bicarbonate of soda and
mix again.

Now knead the gingerbread dough on a
floured work surface until homogeneous
and smooth.

Roll the dough out on the floured work
surface to 2–3mm (⅛in) thick and cut out mini
gingerbread men with a cookie cutter, or you
could use any other mini shape you want.

Bake for 8 minutes, then cool on a wire rack.
They will keep for up to 3 weeks in an airtight
container.

There Is Always Room for Something Sweet

CLASSIC CHOCOLATE CRUNCHY COOKIES

In my family we have something we call *kedelig kiks*: 'boring biscuits'! These biscuits (cookies) are a bit dry, not too sweet and ready to be dunked in tea. I used to bake biscuits that were even more boring, with no sugar, just a splash of apple juice, when I was on one of my more extreme health kicks. I am a bit over that now, but I still love biscuits that are not too sweet. I am also a big fan of dark chocolate, but not too much. Add just a thin layer of it to a *kedelig kiks* and you have this: my favourite afternoon treat.

MAKES 15–16

200g (7oz) wholemeal (wholewheat) flour,
  plus more to dust
50g (1¾oz) small (not jumbo) rolled oats
1 tsp baking powder
40g (1½oz) light brown sugar
1 tsp sea salt flakes (kosher salt)
125g (1 stick plus 1 tbsp) salted butter, chilled
  and chopped
50ml (¼ cup) whole milk

For the chocolate glaze
100g (3½oz) dark chocolate, 70 per cent cocoa
  solids, broken up
1 tsp salted butter

Preheat the oven to 200°C/400°F/Gas Mark 6.

Blitz the flour and oats in a blender, then place in a mixing bowl and stir in the baking powder, sugar and salt. Using your fingertips, rub in the cold butter until the mixture looks like crumbs. Add the milk and knead to form a smooth dough. If the dough feels dry, add a splash of cold water.

Line 2 baking sheets with baking parchment.

Tip the dough out on to a floured work surface, then, using a well-floured rolling pin, roll the dough out to just over 3–4mm (⅛in) thick. Cut into rounds with a 6–7cm (2½–2¾in) cookie cutter, or a similar-sized glass. Keep re-rolling the scraps together to make additional biscuits.

Transfer the biscuits to the prepared sheets and prick them with a fork to create holes, or any kind of pattern. Bake for 10 minutes until pale gold. Transfer to a wire rack to cool.

Now prepare the glaze. Melt the chocolate in a heatproof bowl placed over a saucepan of simmering water, making sure the bowl does not touch the water. Add the butter and stir well. When the biscuits have cooled, spread the chocolate over each. Leave to rest until the chocolate has set.

TRADITIONAL STRAWBERRY-MARZIPAN CAKE

As far as I'm concerned, this cake has got it all: marzipan, chocolate, cream, vanilla and strawberries. It can be found in almost every bakery in Denmark, though the bought cakes vary in quality. You can bake the marzipan base and keep it in the freezer; I like to bake four at a time and keep them, so I can easily assemble this cake on a summer's day.

SERVES 10–12

For the marzipan base
125g (1 stick plus 1 tbsp) salted butter, softened, plus more for the tin
125g (4½oz) good-quality marzipan, with 60 per cent almonds, grated (shredded) (for homemade, see page 220)
125g (4½oz) caster (superfine) sugar
3 eggs
40g (1½oz) cornflour (corn starch)

For the cream
1 vanilla pod (bean)
200ml (generous ¾ cup) single (light) cream
2 egg yolks
3 tbsp caster (superfine) sugar
1 tbsp cornflour (corn starch)
200g (7oz) double (heavy) cream

For the chocolate glaze
200g (7oz) dark chocolate, at least 70 per cent cocoa solids, chopped
4 tbsp double (heavy) cream

For the topping
2–3 tbsp redcurrant jelly
500g (1lb 2oz) strawberries, hulled and halved
edible flowers, such as elderflowers, to decorate (optional)

Preheat the oven to 190°C/375°F/Gas Mark 5. Butter a 24cm (9½in) round cake tin (pan).

Using an electric whisk, beat the grated marzipan with the sugar in a mixing bowl, then add the butter and beat again until smooth. Add the eggs one at a time, beating between additions, until the mixture is even and smooth, then fold in the cornflour. Pour the batter into the prepared tin and bake for 25 minutes. Remove from the oven and allow to cool, then remove from the tin.

Now for the cream. Split the vanilla pod in half lengthways and scrape out the seeds with the tip of a knife. Put the vanilla seeds and the single cream in a small saucepan and heat until steaming hot. Meanwhile, with an electric whisk, whisk the egg yolks and sugar together in a mixing bowl until the mixture turns pale yellow and fluffy, then whisk in the cornflour. Stir one-third of the hot cream into the egg mixture, then pour the egg mixture into the saucepan. Stir over a low heat until it starts to thicken. Remove from the heat and leave to cool. When it is cold, whip the double cream until it forms stiff peaks, then fold it into the custard.

Continued overleaf...

TRADITIONAL STRAWBERRY-MARZIPAN CAKE
CONTINUED . . .

For the glaze, place the chocolate and cream in a heatproof bowl set over a saucepan of simmering water, ensuring the bowl does not touch the water. When the chocolate has melted, remove from the heat, stir briefly to combine, then set aside until slightly cooler.

When the marzipan base has cooled, spread the chocolate glaze evenly over it and allow it to set.

Pile the cream on top of the chocolate, forming it into a dome or pyramid shape that finishes 2cm (1in) from the edge.

Spoon the redcurrant jelly into a piping bag.

Cover the cream with the strawberries, then pipe small dollops of redcurrant jelly in between the strawberries. Decorate with edible flowers, if you like.

Serve right away, or keep in the refrigerator for up to 1 day until you're ready to serve.

RHUBARB MERINGUE CAKE

In Scandinavia, the first rhubarb stalks are a sign of spring; therefore, anything made with rhubarb makes people happy. It is a sign of the new season, a change in the light and the temperature, and the knowledge that fresh produce will shortly emerge from the land.

SERVES 8

For the cake
175g (1¾ sticks) salted butter, plus more
   for the tin
150g (5½oz) caster (superfine) sugar
3 eggs
75g (2¾oz) skin-on almonds
100g (3½oz) plain (all-purpose) flour,
   plus 1 tbsp
2 tsp baking powder
300g (10½oz) rhubarb

For the meringue topping
3 egg whites
200g (7oz) caster (superfine) sugar
1 tsp distilled vinegar, or white wine vinegar

Preheat the oven to 180°C/350°F/Gas Mark 4. Line the base of a 24cm (9½in) round springform cake tin (pan) with baking parchment, then butter the parchment.

Cream the butter and sugar with an electric whisk until light and fluffy. Add the eggs one at a time, beating well after each addition.

Grind the almonds in a food processor until fine. Then, in a small bowl, mix them with the 100g (3½oz) flour and the baking powder.

Add the dry ingredients to the batter gradually, while beating at slow speed, then pour the batter into the prepared tin.

Cut the rhubarb into 1cm (½in) pieces and place in a bowl, then fold in the 1 tbsp flour to coat the pieces well. Spread the floured rhubarb evenly on top of the cake batter. Place in the oven and bake for 25 minutes.

Meanwhile, for the topping, whisk the egg whites with an electric whisk until stiff, but do not overwhisk them. Gradually add the sugar – it should take around 15 minutes – then add the vinegar. Spread the meringue evenly over the cake after it has baked for 25 minutes.

Return the cake to the oven for a final 15 minutes, then take out and allow to cool. Remove from the tin and serve at room temperature.

FLAVOURED EASTER EGGS

I like to make these for Easter in different flavours, though I always also make the classic, with unflavoured, pure marzipan. For these, you have to use good-quality marzipan containing at least 60 per cent almonds. This is pretty hard to find outside of Scandinavia, but it is easy to make, so I have given a recipe here. It scales up very easily, so if you want to make two or three flavours of eggs here (and so will need 600g/1lb 5oz or 900g/2lb of it), simply double or triple all the quantities. You will also need a cooking thermometer to temper the chocolate.

Each recipe here makes 12 eggs. If I want them to last all through Easter, I have to make a double portion, because my husband eats them too fast...

MARZIPAN

MAKES 300g (10½oz)
or *enough for 12 eggs*

250g (9oz) almonds (I prefer skin-on almonds, but use blanched/skinned for white marzipan)
50g (1¾oz) icing (powdered) sugar, plus more to dust
25ml (1fl oz) water

Whizz the almonds in a food processor until they become a paste. Add the icing sugar, whizz again, then add the water and whizz for a final time.

Take the marzipan out of the food processor and knead it on a work surface dusted with icing sugar. Wrap in cling film and store in the refrigerator; it will keep for up to 2 weeks.

CLASSIC EGGS

300g (10½oz) good-quality marzipan, with 60 per cent almonds (for homemade, see above)

For the tempered dark chocolate
250g (9oz) dark chocolate, 70 per cent cocoa solids, finely chopped

Divide the marzipan into 12 pieces of 25g (about 1oz) and roll each into an egg shape. Leave to rest for a few hours, or overnight, at room temperature.

To temper the chocolate, take two-thirds of it and melt very gently in a heatproof bowl set over a saucepan of simmering water, making sure the bowl does not touch the water. Ensure the chocolate doesn't overheat.

Continued overleaf...

There Is Always Room for Something Sweet

When it has melted and has reached 50°C (122°F), add the remaining chocolate and mix until all the chocolate has melted. Heat all the chocolate very gently until it reaches a temperature of about 31°C (88°F). Now the chocolate is ready to be used.

Dip the marzipan eggs in the tempered chocolate and roll them around so they are covered sufficiently, making sure to let the chocolate drip a little, so any excess runs off.

Place on a tray lined with baking parchment. Set aside until the chocolate has set, then store in an airtight tin for up to 3 weeks.

ORANGE EGGS

270g (9½oz) good-quality marzipan, with 60 per
  cent almonds (for homemade, see opposite)
finely grated (shredded) zest of 1 orange
2 tbsp sieved bitter orange marmalade
  (without any pieces of fruit)
200g (7oz) Tempered Dark Chocolate
  (see opposite)

For the candied peel
1 orange
25g (1oz) caster (superfine) sugar

The night before you want to eat the eggs, mix the marzipan with the orange zest and marmalade in a small bowl. Divide it into 12 pieces of 25g (about 1oz) and roll each into an egg shape. Leave to rest for a few hours, or overnight, at room temperature.

For the candied peel, cut the peel off the orange and slice it into at least 12 small strips. Put them in a small saucepan with the sugar and place over a medium heat. Let it cook for 5 minutes. Place a sheet of baking parchment close to the stovetop.

Take the candied orange zest out of the sugar with a fork and let the pieces dry on the baking parchment.

Dip the marzipan eggs in the tempered chocolate and roll them around so they are covered sufficiently, making sure to let the chocolate drip a little, so any excess runs off.

Place on a tray lined with baking parchment and stick a piece of candied orange zest on each. Set aside until the chocolate has set, then store in an airtight tin for up to 3 weeks.

TRIPLE ALMOND EGGS

50g (1¾oz) almonds, plus 2 tbsp chopped
  almonds
300g (10½oz) good-quality marzipan, with 60 per
  cent almonds (for homemade, see page 220)
2 tbsp Amaretto liqueur
250g (9oz) Tempered Dark Chocolate
  (see page 220)

The night before you want to make the eggs,
toast the 50g (1¾oz) almonds in a dry frying
pan (skillet), allow them to cool, then finely
chop them and mix with the marzipan and
Amaretto liqueur in a small bowl. Divide the
mixture into 12 pieces of 25g (about 1oz) and
roll each into an egg shape. Leave to rest for a
few hours, or overnight, at room temperature.

Dip the marzipan eggs in the tempered
chocolate and roll them around so they are
covered sufficiently, making sure to let the
chocolate drip a little, so any excess runs off.

Place on a tray lined with baking parchment
and decorate with the 2 tbsp chopped
almonds. Set aside until the chocolate has set,
then store in an airtight tin for up to 3 weeks.

INDEX

ACKNOWLEDGEMENTS

1000 *TAK og kærlighed* to my family Niels Peter, Kelly, Peter Emil, and Michala for always eating what I cook and loving me as I am. Thanks to my sister Silla Bjerrum for a lifelong exchange of food and knowledge.

Thank you to the team at Hahnemanns Køkken for support and creative input. Huge *TAK* to Kelly Andersen, Cristian Inoita, Meagan Murray and Stine Knudsen for helping out with baking, cooking, chopping and cleaning.

To my publisher, Sarah Lavelle, for still believing I have recipes and stories in me. To my team at Quadrille for producing another beautiful book with me: Harriet Webster, Emily Lapworth and Katy Everett.

Thank you for the wonderful photography, Columbus Leth – we did it again! Thank you Christina Winsløv for always being supportive.

To my dear friends, for their love and always being game to eat with me: Fie Hansen-Hoeck, Lisa Høgh Nielsen, Christina Rosendahl, and Flora.

A special thanks to my agent Heather Holden Brown, and editor Lucy Bannell, for being patient as always.

ABOUT THE AUTHOR

A chef and food writer, Trine Hahnemann
is an enthusiastic advocate for sustainable
solutions, organic sourcing and simple food
cooked with love. With her great knowledge
of Danish food and food culture, she writes
for and appears regularly in the media in
America and Britain. Trine has written
several cookbooks both in her native Danish
and in English, including *Scandinavian Baking*,
Scandinavian Comfort Food, *Copenhagen Food*
(winner of the Guild of Food Writers award
for International or Regional Cookbook) and,
most recently, *Scandinavian Green*.

Managing Director Sarah Lavelle
Commissioning Editor Harriet Webster
Senior Designer Emily Lapworth
Designer Katy Everett
Copy-editor Lucy Bannell
Photographer Columbus Leth
Head of Production Stephen Lang
Senior Production Controller Gary Hayes

Published in 2023 by Quadrille,
an imprint of Hardie Grant Publishing

Quadrille
52–54 Southwark Street
London SE1 1UN
quadrille.com

Cataloguing in Publication Data: a
catalogue record for this book is available
from the British Library.

Text © Trine Hahnemann 2023
Photography © Columbus Leth 2023
Design © Quadrille 2023

ISBN 978 1 78713 901 5

Printed in China